O'Donnells of Tyrconnell

This book is dedicated to my wife Annette,
sons Rory and Colm

Edited by Vincent O'Donnell

O'Donnells of Tyrconnell

A compilation of articles on the history of the O'Donnell Clan
with emphasis on the last four centuries.

Published by
Dálach Publications
Inver
Co. Donegal
00353 749736059

First published 1989 as Clann Dálaigh
2nd Edition 1997 as O'Donnells of Tír Chonaill
2nd Edition reprint 2000.

ISBN 978-0-9555625-0-1

Edited by Vincent O'Donnell

vodonnell@eircom.net

www.odonnellclan.com
© Vincent O'Donnell
No material from this book may be reproduced without permission
from the Publishers.

Printed by Brownes Printers, Port Road, Letterkenny, Co. Donegal.
Tel: 00 353 74 9121387
Fax: 00 353 74 9126638
Email: reception@browneprinters.com

Contents

Sources of O'Donnell Genealogy..5
Rupert S. O Cochlaín...7
Nomenclature..8
A Brief History of the O'Donnells...10
Arms & Name..12
Donegal Castle..15
Iris Oifigúil...16
End of O' Donnell Reign...17
The Newport Line..20
The Larkfield Line...23
The Castlebar Line..26
The Spanish Line..28
The Austrian Line...31
The Glasagh Line..35
The Ramelton Line..40
The Rosses O'Donnells..42
Inauguration of a Chieftan...44
An Cathach...45
The Capture and Escape of Red Hugh...45
Fuadach Aodh Rua..51
Pilleadh Aodh Ruaidh Uí Domhnaill..54
Red Hugh O'Donnells Address..56
Red Hugh's March to Kinsale...59
The Last Will of Red Hugh O'Donnell..62
Death of Aodh Rua..65
Aodh Mac Aodh Dubh of Ramelton...68
Lieutenant General Charles H. O'Donnel...69
Hugh O'Donnell of Larkfield..73
Godfrey O'Donnell..74
The Battle of Farsetmore...76
Manus O'Donnell, 21st Lord of Tyrconnell..78
Mánus A' Phíce...79
To Rome by Boat, Coach and Horseback..84
O'Donnell Participants in the "Flight of the Earls".....................................87
Lament for the Princes of Tyrone and Tyrconnell......................................88
The O'Donnell Name Abroad..89
O'Donnell Abu..91
O'Donnell Dwelling Places...92
Galún Uí Dhomhnaill...93
The Jahrgang O'Donnell..94
Picture Pages..96

FOREWORD

This book has evolved from a book entitled Clann Dálaigh first published in 1989 as a souvenir book for the O'Donnell Clan Gathering of that year. It was a compilation of articles, most of which had already appeared in Ó Domhnaill Abú the O'Donnell Clan newsletter which is being published since 1985 and which deals mainly with the fortune of the mainline family since 1600.

In 1997 the same book was reprinted under the new title O'Donnells of Tír Chonaill with some necessary changes. Both editions are now out of print.

As both of the above contain some minor errors and as many changes have taken place in the O'Donnell world since 1989, and indeed new information has come to light, it was felt that a re-vamp was necessary; hence this book.

We, the O'Donnells, are fortunate in that we have always had excellent chroniclers to record the deeds and genealogy of our clan, and to them we must be grateful. It is due to people like Lughaidh O'Clery, the Four Masters, John O'Donovan, Charles Joseph O'Donnell of Castlebar, members of the Spanish and Austrian families and to the late Rupert S.O Cochláin (to whom this book is dedicated and from whom much of the material was received) that the O'Donnells are probably the best documented of all Irish Clans. This was apparent at the Young Ireland Book Show held in the Mansion House, Dublin in 1945; when the Genealogical Office was asked for an exhibit, it submitted the O'Donnell pedigree.

I wish to express my gratitude to all those who helped in any way to make this book possible – those who contributed articles, Rupert S. Ó Cochláin R.I.P., Séamus Mac Aoidh R.I.P., Eunan O'Donnell; those who contributed photos and information, members of the Spanish and Austrian O'Donnels, Charles Farkas, Rupert S. Ó Cochláin; Chris Campbell who did the proofreading and anybody else that I've forgotten.

While the author has gone to great lengths to ensure correct facts, literacy may have suffered; please forgive. And as at present, books on the history of Clann Dálaigh are few or non existent, it is hoped that this humble offering might fill the void until better becomes available.

Vincent O'Donnell
March 2007.

Sources of O'Donnell Genealogy

by Rupert S. O'Cochláin

The following is a general guide to the genealogies of the O'Donnells. The list is not exhaustive.

'O'Clery Book of Genealogies'(Royal Irish Academy MS. 23 D 17), transcribed by Cuchoigcrice Ó Cléirigh, who lived into the 1660's. It has been edited and published by Seamus Pender, M.A. for the Irish Manuscripts Commission in Analecta Hibernica No. 18(1951).

O'Fearral's 'Linea Antiqua,' original in the Genealogical Office, Dublin, copy in the National Library.

Dubhaltach MacFirbhisigh, 'Book of Genealogies,' in University College, Dublin.

Annals of the Four Masters.

Calendars of State Papers (Ireland).

Seathrún Céitinn, 'Foras Feasa ar Éirinn,' edited Rev. Patrick Dinneen, M.A., for Irish Text Society, Vol. XV (1914).

Tadhg Ó Cianáin, 'The Flight of the Earls,' edited Rev. Paul Walsh, M.A., (1916).

Tadhg Ó Cianáin, 'Imeacht na nIarlaí,' edited Pádraig de Barra and Tomás Ó Fiach. (1972).

Seamus Maguidhir, 'Dunaire Uí Dhómhnaill,' National Library MS. 167.

Lughaidh Ó Cléirigh, 'Beatha Aodh Ruaidh Uí Dhómhnaill,' edited Rev. Denis Murphy, S.J., (1895).

Ibid, edited Rev. Paul Walsh, 2 Vols. for Irish Text Society.

John O'Donovan, Appendix to the Annals of the Four Masters.

John O'Donovan, 'The O'Donnells in Exile,' 'Duffy's Hibernian Magazine,' Vol. 1, December 1860.

Sir Bernard Burke, LL.D, 'A Genealogical History of the Dormant, Abeyant, Forfeited and Extinct Peerages,' (1866).

Justus Perthes, 'Grafl Taschenbuch,' (1901).

Rev. Paul Walsh, 'O'Donnell Genealogies' Analecta Hibernica No. 8 March, 1938. These are also incorporated in Vol. II of No. 11 above.

Micheline Walsh, 'Spanish Knights of Irish Origin,' 4 Vols. Irish Manuscripts Commission.

John O'Hart, 'Irish Pedigrees.'

Pádraic Ó Domhnaill, 'The O'Donnells of Newport House and the Execution of Fr. Sweeney,' Western People (c. 1934).

Pádraig Ó Moráin, 'Annala Beaga Bhuiris Umhaill,' (1960).

Espasa, a Spanish Dictionary of Biography.

Dr. Christian Sapper, Vienna, unpublished Ph.D. thesis, 'Die Familia O'Donnell in Österrich,' (1977). Copy in writer's collection.

Genealogical Office, various pedigrees.

Synopsis Genealogiae, prepared 1767 and sent to Branches of the family in Spain and Austria. Copy in writer's collection.

O'Donnell Pedigree registered in Royal Herald of Arms, Brussels, 1773. Original in possession of Count O'Donel von Tyrconnell of Austria. Copy in writer's collection.

O'Donnell Pedigree registered Vienna, 1782, ditto.

Charles Joseph O'Donel (1818-1901), O'Donnell Pedigree prepared by. Original in Überacker-O'Donell Archives, Austria. Copy in writer's collection.

Joseph O'Donnell y Lestache, Pedigree of Spanish Branch of family (1871). Original in writer's collection.

Prof. O'Donel-Alexander, O'Donnell Pedigree prepared by, 1911-12. Original in possession of C.H. O'Donel-Alexander, O.B.E., London. Copy in writer's collection.

Blanca O'Donnell y Mendoza, Duchess of Tetuan, Pedigree of Spanish Branch prepared by, 1951. Original in writer's collection.

Rupert S. Ó Cochláin, Pedigree of the Austrian O'Donnells prepared by, 1959.

Alfonso O'Donnell y Lara, Pedigree of Spanish Branch prepared by, 1971. Copy in writer's collection.

Rupert S. Ó Cochláin

by V. O'Donnell

A native of Co. Cork, his first post as a Civil Servant was in the Rosses area of Co. Donegal where he took a keen interest in Clann Dálaigh. He married Roisín O'Donnell, a Rosses woman, which possibly increased his interest in the Clan. For over 45 years he left no stone unturned in his inexhaustible quest for information on the O'Donnell Clan. Early in his career he re-established communications with the Austrian and Spanish Branches. This communication had lapsed since the death of Charles Joseph O'Donel (57) in 1901. He was welcomed by both families and given access to their archives. While posted to Dublin he spent all his free time doing research in the National Library, Dublin Castle and other such places. He wrote and lectured on the topic to the Military History Society and the Donegal Historical Society both of which he was a member.

I had the privilege and pleasure of spending many hours with him learning and assisting. I marveled at his knowledge and memory, his meticulous record keeping, his never-ending letter-writing and above all the amount and quality of material on the O'Donnell Clan he had amassed. Much of what is contained in this publication is due to his untiring research. His soul departed this world on the 18th May 1986 at the age of 78.   Ar Dheis Dé go raibh a anam.

NOMENCLATURE

by V. O'Donnell

To those unfamiliar with the Gaelic language and how names, both of people and of places, became anglicized, the following is intended. Once upon a time when only the Gaelic language was spoken in Ireland things were simple except for spelling which hadn't been standardised. But as the English language encroached and finally dominated, proper names became anglicized for two reasons`- firstly because the foreigners had problems with the pronunciation and secondly it was their policy to make Ireland a British colony and to that end it was important that they remove all vestiges of the Gaelic civilisation. Seemingly, there were no standards set and so the anglecised versions and their spelling vary. In some cases the transformation was phonetical e.g. Eoghan Rua > Owen Roe, while in other cases an English variant was used, e.g. Aodh Rua > Red Hugh.

Some family names such as Ó Baoighill, Ó Dochartaigh, Ó Gallchobhair became O'Boyle, O'Doherty, O'Gallagher but the 'O' was still considered Gaelic and was eventually dropped.

Here follows some names, regularly appearing in Donegal history, along with their anglecised forms -

Aedh, Aodh = Hugh
Cathbhar = Caffar, Caffer
Donal, Domhnall = Donnell, Daniel
Niall = Neal, Nial
Seán = Shane, John
Mánus, Maghnus = Manus
Calbhach = Calvagh
Ruadhraí = Rory, Rury
Conall = Con, Conn, Connell
Gofraigh - Godfrey
Feidhlimí = Felim
Dubh = Black, Duv, Duff (black, dark)
Rua = Red, Roe (hair, complexion)
Óg = Oge (young, junior)
Mór = More (big, great, senior)
Beag = Beg (small, junior)
Buí = Boy (yellow)
Garbh = Garve (rough)

Ó Néill = O'Neill
Ó Domhnaill = O'Donnell
Ó Ruairc = O'Rourke
Mac Suibhne = MacSwine, Mac Sweeney, Sweeney
Mac an Bháird = Ward
Mac Uidhir = Maguire
Ó Cléirigh - O'Cleary, Clarke
Ua, Ó = O (grandson or descendant of)
Ní = (granddaughter or descendant of)
Mac = Mac, Mc (son or descendant of)
Nic = (daughter or descendant of)
Tír Chonaill = Tyrconnell (Land of Connell)
Tír Eoghain = Tyrone (Land of Owen)

HUGH MAC CAFFER = Hugh, son of Caffer (in this case 'Mac Caffer' is not a surname but denotes relationship, likewise DONAL MAC DONAL O'DONNELL = Donal, son of Donal O'Donnell;)
was no clear-cut policy regarding the anglicisation of personal names nor no standard spelling, that was left to whatever official happened to be writing or recording it. Thus one Gaelic surname may have several English versions e.g. Mac Aodh = McHugh, Magee or McGee; Mac Ruaidhri = McGrory, Magroary or Rodgers

Aodh Dubh d.1537 (1)

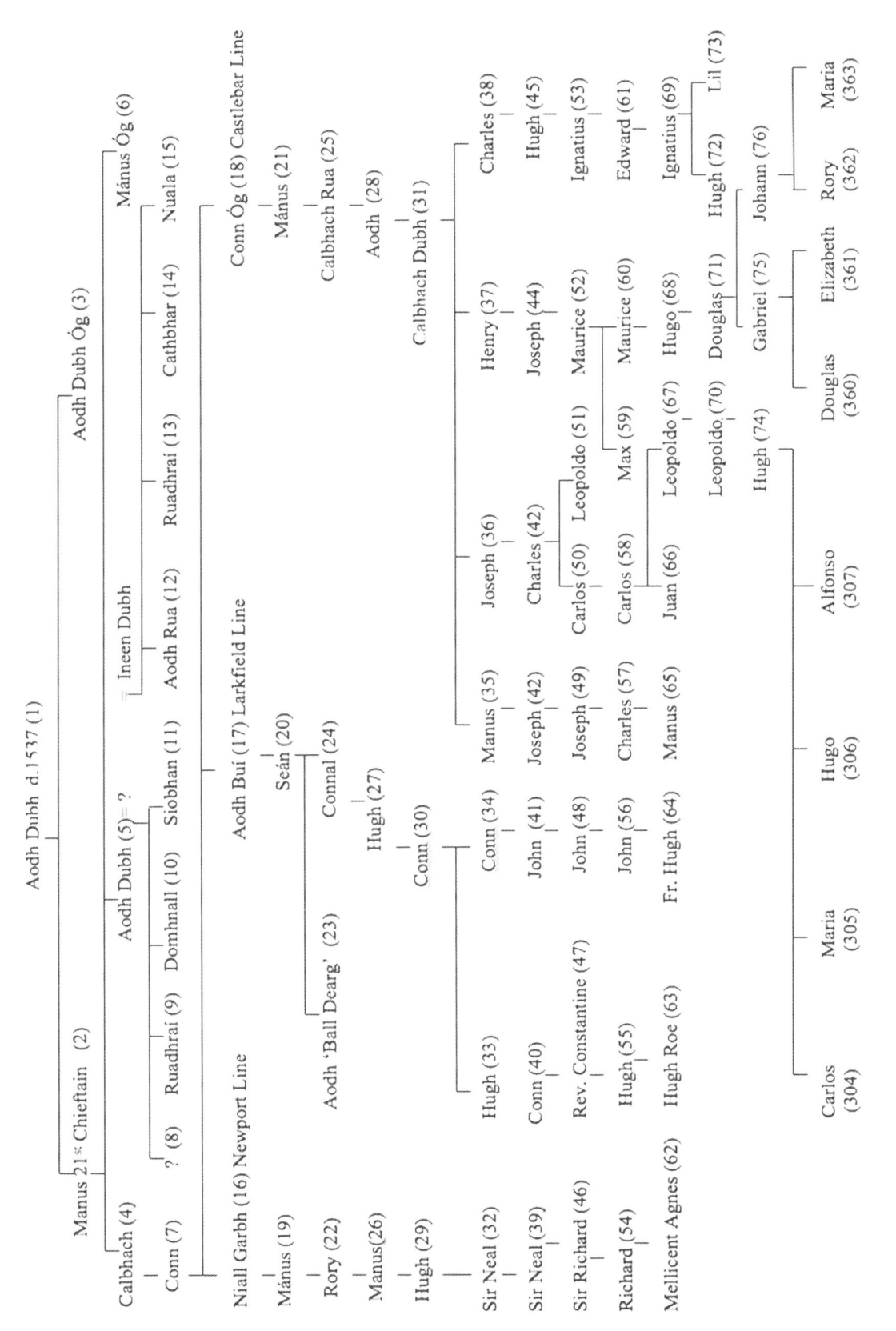

Manus 21ˢᵗ Chieftain (2)

Aodh Dubh Óg (3)

Aodh Dubh (5) = ?   Ineen Dubh

Calbhach (4)
Ruadhraí (9)
Domhnall (10)
Siobhan (11)
Aodh Rua (12)
Ruadhraí (13)
Cathbhar (14)
Nuala (15)
Mánus Óg (6)

Conn (7)
? (8)

Niall Garbh (16) Newport Line
Aodh Buí (17) Larkfield Line
Conn Óg (18) Castlebar Line

Mánus (19)
Seán (20)
Mánus (21)

Rory (22)
Aodh 'Ball Dearg' (23)
Connal (24)
Calbhach Rua (25)

Manus (26)
Hugh (27)
Aodh (28)

Hugh (29)
Conn (30)
Calbhach Dubh (31)

Sir Neal (32)
Hugh (33)
Conn (34)
Manus (35)
Joseph (36)
Henry (37)
Charles (38)

Sir Neal (39)
Conn (40)
John (41)
Joseph (42)
Charles (42)
Joseph (44)
Hugh (45)

Sir Richard (46)
Rev. Constantine (47)
John (48)
Joseph (49)
Carlos (50)
Leopoldo (51)
Maurice (52)
Ignatius (53)

Richard (54)
Hugh (55)
John (56)
Charles (57)
Carlos (58)
Max (59)
Maurice (60)
Edward (61)

Mellicent Agnes (62)
Hugh Roe (63)
Fr. Hugh (64)
Manus (65)
Juan (66)
Leopoldo (67)
Hugo (68)
Ignatius (69)

Leopoldo (70)
Douglas (71)
Hugh (72)
Lil (73)

Hugh (74)
Gabriel (75)
Johann (76)

Carlos (304)
Maria (305)
Hugo (306)
Alfonso (307)

Douglas (360)
Elizabeth (361)
Rory (362)
Maria (363)

9

A Brief History of the O'Donnells (Clann Dálaigh)

by V. O'Donnell

About 1700 years B.C., Milesius, then king of Spain, planned an invasion of Ireland. He died, however, before he could carry out his plan but his two sons, Eber and Eremon, saw it through. They disagreed, however, as to which of them should rule and finally settled the argument by dividing the country between them. This did not seem to be satisfactory as Eber was later killed by his brother. Thus, Eremon became king of all Ireland.

On top of Doon Rock(inauguration site of the O'Donnells) during the 1954 Clan Gathering. Centre, with the 'Slat Bhán' is John O'Donel then head of Clann Dálaigh. Far right, his son Hugh (64). Far left, Gabriel Count O'Donell von Tyrconnell (75). Photo supplied by Rupert O'Cochláin whose wife, Róisín, stands next to John.

Niall of the Nine Hostages (Nial Naoi nGiallach) who reigned from 379-405 A.D. and is reputed as having brought St. Patrick to Ireland as a slave boy, was the 52nd lineal descendant of Eremon.
Niall had many sons among whom was Eoghan, ancestor of the O'Neills (Cineal Eoghain) and Conall, ancestor of the O'Donnells (Cineal Chonaill).
Conall asserted his dominance over that territory which became known as 'Tír Chonaill' (approx. Co. Donegal minus Inishown). Among Conall's descendants were no fewer than 41 Saints, 10 High Kings and a host of lesser nobility.

Around the year 1000 A.D. Brian Boru, then High King, ordered that families take surnames. The practice before that was for a person to add the name of his father or grandfather to that of his own, a practice which still exists in some parts of Ireland today.

The change was gradual and it was not until a century later that the surname 'Ó Domhnaill' (O'Donnell) appeared when Cathbharr (d. 1106) adopted the name of his ancestor - Domhnall Mór- as his surname. (There is an entry in the Annals of the Four Masters for the year 1010 that reads - 'Maelruanaidh Ua Domhnaill, lord of Cinel Luighdheach, was slain by the men of Magh Ith.' But this is not officially accepted as a surname.)

Another clan in the Clare/Tipperary area adopted the same surname but from a different ancestor, of course. This was long before Cineal Chonaill did and sometimes causes confusion and misunderstandings. It is difficult to tell whether a southern O'Donnell is a descendant of the Clare/Tipperary clan or a northern O'Donnell who 'lost his way' on his journey to or from Kinsale, although DNA testing should go along way to show the difference.

About the year 1200A.D. Eighneachan was inaugurated as the first 'Ó Domhnaill' (Chief of the O'Donnells). Twenty five others were to follow; ending with Niall Garbh in 1603. The inauguration ceremony, which took place at Kilmacrennan, had both a lay and a religious side to it.

The O'Donnells first lived along the Lennon River. They had a lake dwelling or Crannóg in Lough Gartan and, later, their first permanent home at Ramelton. Later still, they established themselves at Murvagh on the Erne. At the beginning of the 15th century they built a castle at Ballyshannon and 50 years later built one in Donegal Town. The latter lay in ruins for a few centuries but was restored towards the end of the 20th century. Today it is a thriving visitor centre.

The prominent role played by this royal family in their country's history is well recorded but after their overthrow by the English and the collapse of the old Gaelic order in 1602 (Battle of Kinsale) less is known of them.

The main family immigrated to the Continent in 1607 (Flight of the Earls) where all were to die within a short period of time - the last dying in 1642. Other branches of the family were moved to Connaught during the Cromwellian plantations. About the middle of the 18th century some of these immigrated to Spain and Austria, in which countries they and their descendants were to play an important role.

The most senior O'Donnell family today (according to the office of the Chief Herald) is that of John O'Donel (deceased), Blackrock, Co. Dublin, namely Fr. Hugh O.F.M., Nuala and Siobhan. Thus Fr. Hugh, a Franciscan Friar, at present on the Zimbabwe mission, is head of the O'Donnells. Next in seniority is Hugo O'Donnell, Duke de Tetuan, Madrid, Spain. The next in line, Douglas Count O'Donel von Tyrconnell, lives near Salzburg in Austria.

There are, undoubtedly, other descendants of the noble house of Tyrconnell but absence of proof prevents their genealogy from being determined.

[Source: Na Dálaigh by Rupert S. O Cochlain in Donegal Annual 1950]

ARMS AND NAME

Variations of the Name: (English) O'Donnell, O'Donell, O'Donel, (Gaelic) Ó Domhnaill, Ó Dónaill

Meaning of the Coat of Arms: 'The ancient armorial bearings of the O'Donnells are: Or issuing from sinister side of shield an arm dexter, sleeved azure, and cuffed argent, with hand proper grasping a passion cross gules.

Tradition has it that St. Patrick upon meeting Conall Cremhthainn, an elder son of King Niall(of the Nine Hostages), impressed a cross upon his shield, with his staff(Bachall Isa) promising and predicting that such of his race as would carry that sign on their standard should never be overcome in battle, The family motto is of course 'IN HOC SIGNO VINCES' meaning 'under this sign you will conquer'.

There are many variations of these arms.

It is important to note that for some time before Domhnail Mór's name was accepted as the official surname, as reported elsewhere in this book, many clan members were unofficially using that of Dálach, a former chieftain slain in 868. The latter is still used in Gaelic in the following cases - O'Donnell Clan = Clann Dálaigh; The O'Donnell = An Dálach; The O'Donnells = Na Dálaigh.

Meaning of the Name: Domhan is the Gaelic for 'world' and Domhnall means 'world ruler' or 'world mighty'. Ó Domhnaill = descendent of Domhnall.

Red Hugh O'Donnell's (Aodh Ó Domhnaill) (12) signature as it appears on letters to King Philip of Spain.

—CHIEFTAINS—A.D. 1200-1625

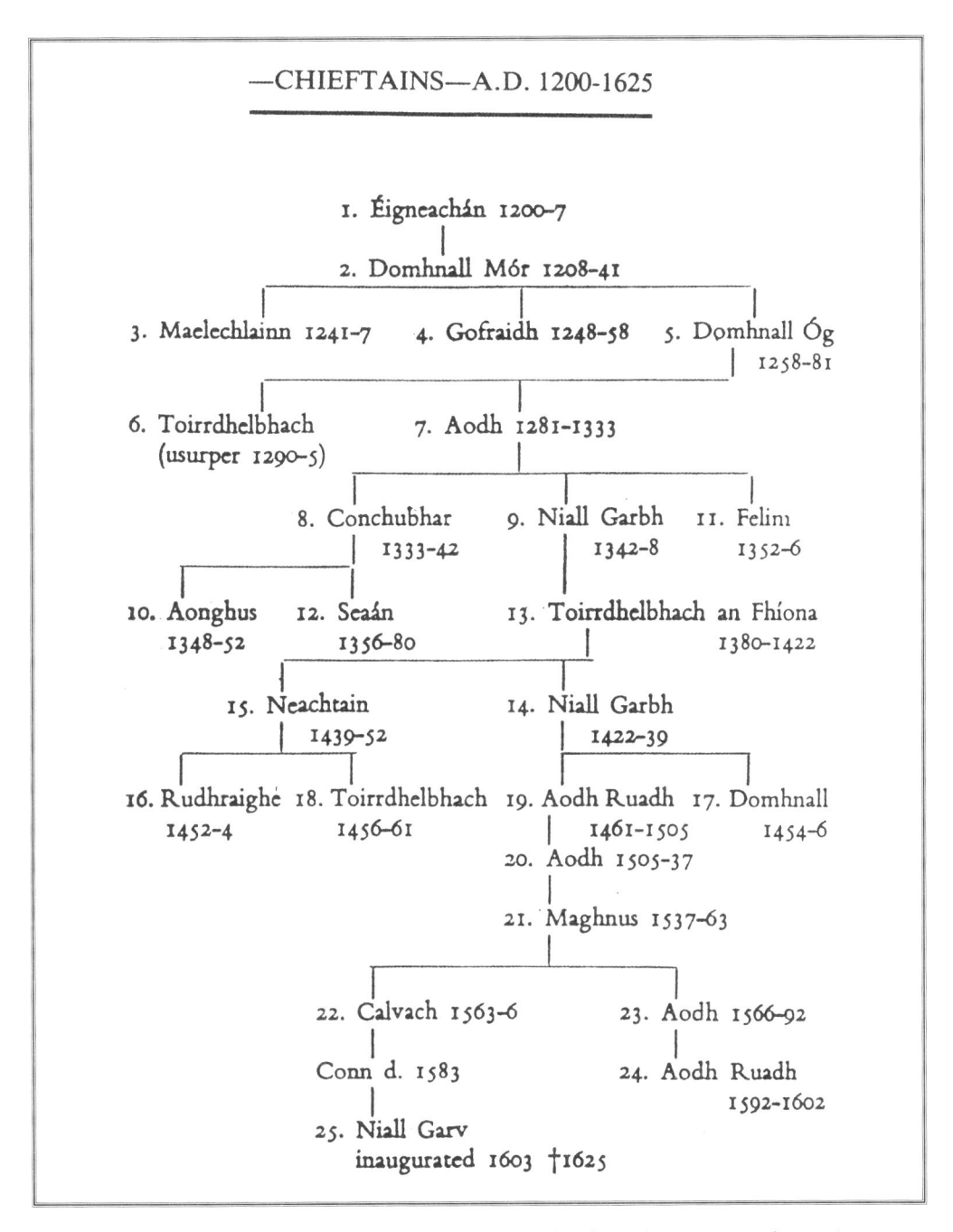

```
                        1. Éigneachán 1200-7
                                 │
                        2. Domhnall Mór 1208-41
        ┌────────────────────────┼────────────────────────┐
3. Maelechlainn 1241-7    4. Gofraidh 1248-58      5. Domhnall Óg
        │                        │                         1258-81
        │                        │
6. Toirrdhelbhach          7. Aodh 1281-1333
  (usurper 1290-5)
                ┌────────────────┼────────────────┐
           8. Conchubhar   9. Niall Garbh     11. Felim
                │              1342-8             1352-6
        ┌───────┴───────┐              │
  10. Aonghus    12. Seaán      13. Toirrdhelbhach an Fhíona
     1348-52       1356-80              │         1380-1422
                     │                  │
              15. Neachtain        14. Niall Garbh
                   1439-52             1422-39
        ┌───────────┼─────────┐    ┌───────────┬──────────┐
16. Rudhraighe  18. Toirrdhelbhach  19. Aodh Ruadh   17. Domhnall
    1452-4         1456-61             1461-1505       1454-6
                                         │
                                   20. Aodh 1505-37
                                         │
                                   21. Maghnus 1537-63
                            ┌────────────┴────────────┐
                      22. Calvach 1563-6         23. Aodh 1566-92
                            │                         │
                       Conn d. 1583             24. Aodh Ruadh
                            │                        1592-1602
                      25. Niall Garv
                      inaugurated 1603 †1625
```

List of O'Donnell Chieftains from Eighneachán, the first (inaugurated 1200) to Niall Garbh, the last (inaugurated 1603 and died in the Tower of London 1626.) One is omitted, namely Conn, who reigned for six months during 1496. His father, Aodh Rua, was Chieftain from 1461-1497 and again from 1497-1505.

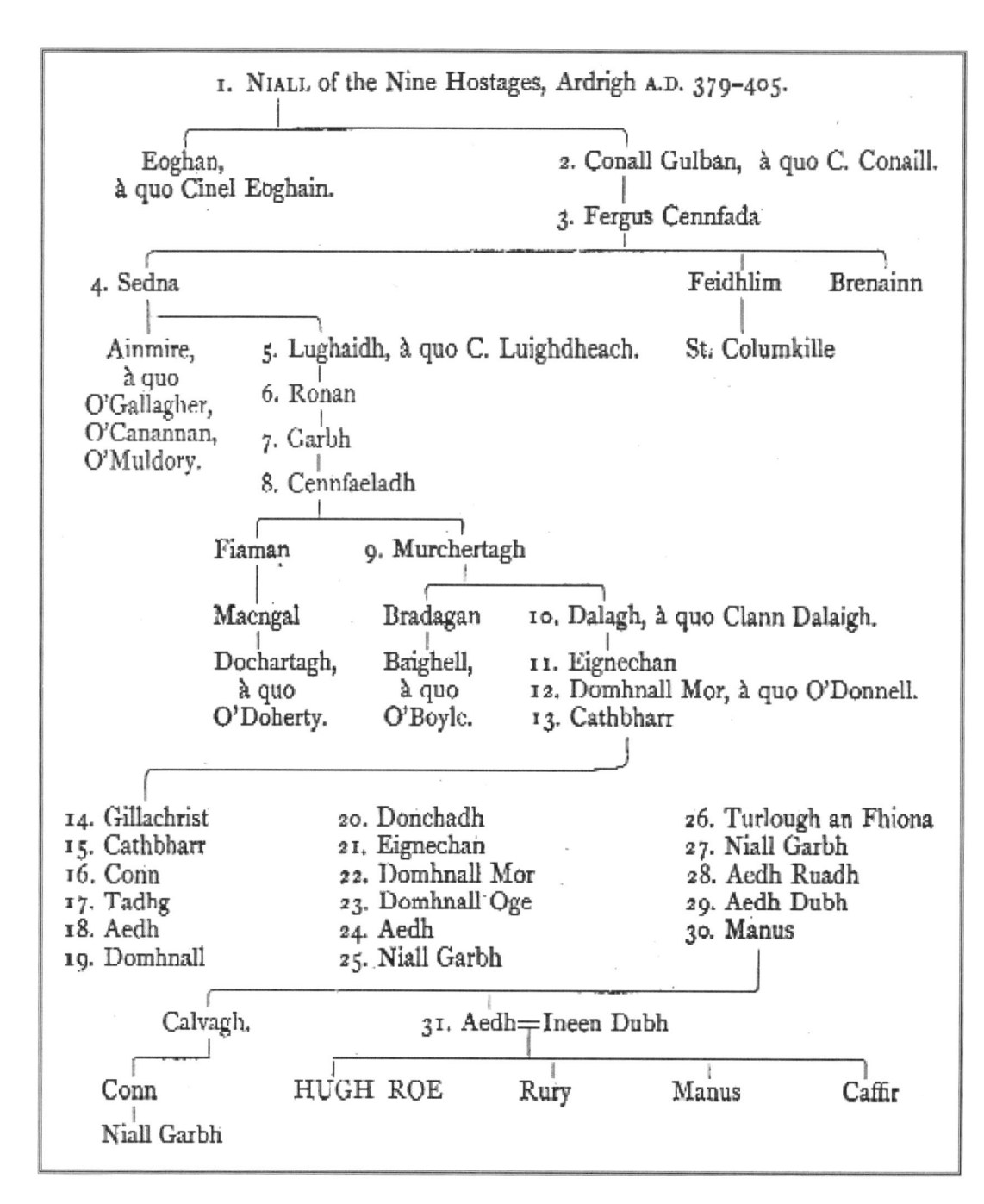

```
                    1. NIALL of the Nine Hostages, Ardrigh A.D. 379-405.
                                            |
        Eoghan,                                      2. Conall Gulban, à quo C. Conaill.
    à quo Cinel Eoghain.                                            |
                                                       3. Fergus Cennfada
                                                              |
   4. Sedna                                              Feidhlim      Brenainn
        |                                                    |
  Ainmire,       5. Lughaidh, à quo C. Luighdheach.    St. Columkille
   à quo              |
 O'Gallagher,    6. Ronan
 O'Canannan,         |
 O'Muldory.      7. Garbh
                     |
                 8. Cennfaeladh
                        |
          Fiaman        9. Murchertagh
            |                 |
          Macngal      Bradagan       10. Dalagh, à quo Clann Dalaigh.
            |             |                  |
         Dochartagh,   Baighell,       11. Eignechan
          à quo         à quo          12. Domhnall Mor, à quo O'Donnell.
         O'Doherty.    O'Boyle.        13. Cathbharr
```

14. Gillachrist	20. Donchadh	26. Turlough an Fhiona
15. Cathbharr	21. Eignechan	27. Niall Garbh
16. Conn	22. Domhnall Mor	28. Aedh Ruadh
17. Tadhg	23. Domhnall Oge	29. Aedh Dubh
18. Aedh	24. Aedh	30. Manus
19. Domhnall	25. Niall Garbh	

```
        Calvagh.              31. Aedh=Ineen Dubh
           |                           |
         Conn           HUGH ROE    Rury    Manus    Caffir
           |
      Niall Garbh
```

This chart shows the lineal descent of Red Hugh (12) (Hugh Roe) d.1602 as well as the origin of Cineal Chonaill i.e. O'Gallagher, O'Boyle, O'Doherty etc

Donegal Castle

by V. O'Donnell

Donegal Castle 200 years ago.

The first Red Hugh O'Donnell, who died in 1505 in the 78th year of his life, is recorded as having built a castle for himself and a convent for the Franciscan Order in Donegal. It is known that the convent or friary was built in 1474 and it is likely that the castle was built about the same time.
It was built in Norman style and masons from England were employed. Tradition has it that animal blood was used in the mortar. Tenants were asked to supply this blood from their animals. Tradition also has it that a widow was annoyed because she was asked to supply blood on more than one occasion. She complained to O'Donnell saying he was hard on his own relatives. He asked her what was the relation and she replied, 'cousins sixteen times removed.' O'Donnell maintained it was so far removed that it was not worth talking about whereupon the woman took a pail and filled in sixteen measures of water (some say milk) and one of blood. The water immediately changed colour. On seeing this, O'Donnell exempted the widow.
Sir Henry Sydney, an English deputy writing of a visit to Donegal in 1566, says of O'Donnell's castle: 'It is the greatest I ever saw in Ireland and in an Irishman's hands and would appear to be in good keeping; one of the fairest situated in good soil and so nigh a portable water as a boat of ten tons could come within twenty yards of it.'
The castle was partially destroyed at the close of the 16th century. This was done on Red Hugh O'Donnell's (12) orders as he realized the danger of the castle falling into enemy hands.

The castle did fall into enemy hands and was granted to Captain Basil Brooke, an English soldier, who had it repaired and extensions added.

The Brooke family is believed to have lived in it up to the opening decade of the 18th century when they moved to Brookhill which they had built. The castle was knocked about during the Williamite Wars.

To-day it is a national monument in the care of the Office of Public Works under whose supervision repairs have been carried out down the years and finally the O'Donnell Tower (the original part of the castle) was fully restored and opened to visitors in 1996.

The official announcement by the Chief Herald, Dr. Edward MacLysaght in the 'Iris Oifigiúl' of the 11th September 1945 proclaiming John O'Donel (56) of the Larkfield Branch head of Clann Dálaigh.

IRIS OIFIGIÚIL, SEPTEMBER 11, 1945

OIFIG GHINEALAIS

Mar thuille leis an liosta ainmneacha a foillsigheadh in Iris Oifigiúil an 22ú de Mhí na Nodlag, 1944, táthar tar éis ainmneacha na ndaoine seo leanas do chur ar an gClár mar thaoisigh dháil na h-ainme

    Mac Murchadha: Major Arthur Thomas MacMurrough Kavanagh, Borris House, Co. Carlow.

    Ó Briain: Sir Donough Edward Foster O Brien, Bart., 16th Baron Inchinquinn, Dromoland Castle, Newmarket-on-Fergus Co. Clare.

    Ó Domhnaill, Clann Dálaigh: O Donnell of Tyrconnell. John O Donel, 37 Seapoint Avenue, Monkstown, Co Dublin.

        EAMONN MAC GIOLLAIASACHTA,
            Príomh-Oifigeach Geinealais.

END OF O' DONNELL REIGN

by V. O'Donnell

When Manus (2) died in 1563 his son Calbhach (4) succeeded him but his term as Chieftain was short lived as he died in 1566. Aodh Dubh (5), Calbhach's brother, contested the Chieftainship with Calbhach's son, Conn (7) and held it against him. This didn't please Calbhach's descendants as the title had now passed to a junior branch of the family.
Aodh Dubh was married twice, firstly to an Irish lady whose name we do not know and secondly to a Scottish lady - Finola, daughter of James McDonnell, Lord of the Isles. Finola was affectionately known as 'Ineen Dubh', the Dark Maiden.
The deaths of two of the first family are recorded in the Annals viz. Rory (9) killed defending Donegal in 1573 d.s.p., and Domhnall (10) slain at the battle of Doire Leathan in 1590. He had a son, Domhnall Óg who participated in the 'Flight' in 1607. In the Calendar of State Papers under date 1592, there is a reference to a boy (8) who is said to have been, "strong in the opinion of the country because he is the eldest son and by an Irishwoman." Apart from a few such vague references, all we have about him is tradition. There was one daughter, Siobhan, who married Hugh O'Neill, Earl of Tyrone, but died shortly afterwards. They had two sons - Hugh who accompanied his father to the Continent and died there in 1609 at the age of 24 and Henry who remained in Ireland and died without issue.
The first born of the second marriage was Aodh Rua (12), the famous Red Hugh who was kidnapped at the age of 16 and held prisoner in Dublin Castle until his successful escape in January 1592. He and Hugh O'Neill fought the Nine Years War against the English until the defeat of Kinsale in 1602 after which he went to Spain to seek help and died there in September 1602 at the age of 30.
His death was a terrible blow to Ireland. A great hero and leader was lost and furthermore, there was little hope of Spanish aid. Whatever morale existed in Ulster now faded. Rory (13) who was left in charge during Aodh's absence suddenly found himself in a hopeless situation and realized that the best course of action was to sue for peace. Under the terms of this agreement Rory was forced to give up much of his territory to the Crown, O'Doherty and Niall Garbh (16). He lost Ballymote Castle and had to renounce his lordship outside the geographical area of Tyrconnell. He was compelled to accept the English title 'Earl of Tyrconnell' instead of the traditional Irish one, 'Ó Domhnaill'.

Life for Rory became very difficult. With the loss of so much of his territories his revenues were greatly diminished. He was constantly watched by English agents. False rumours were being spread and malicious deeds perpetrated by those who coveted his lands. It soon became quite clear to both himself and to Hugh O'Neill that their lives were in danger and their only hope for survival was to leave the country until such time as they could return with foreign aid. Plans were made. A ship and crew were procured and on the 14th September 1607 they sailed down Lough Swilley, around the north west coast, south to Clew Bay and out into the Atlantic to avoid the English warships at Galway. So well planned was their departure and so loyal those who aided them that they were well gone before the English became aware of it.
Rory was married to Bridget Fitzgerald, daughter of the 12th Earl of Kildare and they had a one year old son, Hugh. The latter went with his father on that fateful voyage but Bridget did-

n't as she was visiting her family at the time and expecting their second child.

On arrival on the Continent, the boy Hugh was befriended by the Archduke Albert, Governor of the Low Countries who granted him a pension and as he grew up had him attached as a page to the Court of the Infanta Isabella at Brussels. Hugh took his benefactor's name in confirmation and is since known as 'Hugh Albert'. He completed his studies at the University of Louvain, joined the Spanish service and rose to the rank of Major General. He was recognized as 'The O'Donnell' on the Continent and in one place is described as 'O' Donnell, Earl of Tyrconnell, Baron of Lifford, Lord of Lower Connaught and Sligo and Knight of the Order of Alacantara'. He desired to return to Ireland at the outbreak of the Confederate Wars but was sent instead to the Mediterranean where he was drowned in an engagement against the French in the summer of 1642. He left no male issue.

His sister, Mary, was born in Ireland after the 'Flight' of 1607. She was brought up in the old faith by her mother. Her grandmother, the Dowager Countess of Kildare, introduced her to the English Court when she was twelve. The King bestowed a large sum of money on her and gave her the name 'Mary Stuart', possibly as restitution for the harsh treatment received by her father. Her grandmother too named her as her heir. Needless to say, Mary had many suitors and every inducement was held out to her to renounce her religion and marry one of the Protestant nobility. This she refused to do and so incurred the displeasure of those in high places. Gradually she fell into disfavour and soon it became clear to her that her future was precarious. Disguised as a cavalier she fled to Flanders. By now her fame had spread to Europe and even Pope Urban VIII commended her stand in defence of her religion.

She eventually married an Irishman, Don John Edward O'Gallagher by whom she had two children, both dying in infancy. Not much is heard of her after that and eventually she fades into obscurity.

But what of Earl Rory? He, along with others, made their way to Rome where they were welcomed by the Pope, given accommodation and a pension. They intended going to Spain, but on arrival on the Continent learned that a peace treaty had been signed between that country and England, and it would have been inappropriate for Spain to harbour the King's enemies.

It soon became clear that there was little hope of realizing their dream of returning with foreign aid and that the future promised only life in exile. This along with their strange environment and the Italian climate took its toll. Rory died on the 28th July 1608 at the age of 33, his brother Cathbharr (14) died within two months. Both were buried with due honours in the Church of San Pietro de Montorio in Rome.

Cathbharr was married to Róise O'Doherty of the ruling house of Inishowen. They had a son, Hugh, who went on the 'Flight'. He died in 1623. Róise later married Eoghan Roe O'Neill.

Nuala (15) also went on the 'Flight'. She had married Niall Garbh (16) but deserted him when he so treacherously went over to the English and cam-

Rory's Grave

paigned against her brother, Aodh Rua (12).

As already said, Calbhach's descendants weren't pleased with the Chieftainship passing to a junior branch and the English were quick to use this to their own advantage. They offered to help Nial Garbh regain the Chieftainship. He accepted and with their help waged a ruthless campaign against Aodh Rua. Nial was knighted in 1602, but when Aodh Rua died in 1602 he went to the Rock of Doon and had himself unofficially inaugurated 'Ó Domhnaill', an action which didn't please the English. He began to fall out of favour and finally in 1608 was accused of being implicated in Cahir O'Doherty's ill-fated rising, arrested and imprisoned in the Tower of London where he died in 1626.

Nial Garbh had two sons, Manus (19) and Neachtan (19a). Neachtan was sent to the Tower along with his father where he spent the remainder of his life. Manus was a Colonel in the Irish army and was killed at the Battle of Benburb in 1646. It is from him that the Newport O'Donnells are descended.

[Source: Na Dálaigh by Rupert S. O Cochlain in Donegal Annual 1950]

Rory's Earl Patent now in possession of Douglas Count O'Donell von Tyrconnell, Austria.

The Newport Line

by V. O'Donnell

Colonel Manus (19) who died at the Battle of Benburb 1646 had a son Rory (22). The latter, known as 'Rory of Lifford', along with a large number of his followers, was forced to move to Connaught during the Cromwellian Plantation. They settled around the Ballycroy area of Co. Mayo sometime prior to 1664 where their descendants are still known as 'Na h-Ultaigh'.

Rory had a son, Manus (26) who was also a colonel in the Irish Army and fought against William at the Boyne and at Aughrim. He lived at Ballycroy at first, but in 1704 when he went surety for several priests at the time of their registration, his address was Rosturk beside Newport. The Colonel was a man of distinction and is the subject of a poem by Cathaoir Mac Caba in which the year of his death is given as 1736.

Manus (26) was married to Eleanor, daughter of Robert Maguire, Chief of Fermanagh and had five of a family – Charles or Calbhach Rua (29a) died 1770; Hugh of Newport (29) died 1762; Manus (29b) d.s.p. 1767; Mary (29c) and Anne (29d). A romantic story involving the last mentioned is worth recounting here. A certain Henry McDermot was engaged to a Miss O'Malley from Mayo. Henry and his mother visited the O'Malley's to make the final wedding arrangements. No sooner had they arrived than Henry asked leave of his mother to visit the house of Manus O'Donnell. She consented on condition that he would return in time for dinner. On his arrival at O'Donnell's he found O'Carolan the harper there. Wine and music flowed freely. With all the merriment Henry forgot his promise and stayed the night. Next morning the priest was sent for and Anne and Henry were married.

Charles (29a) had three sons – Manus, Conn and Lewis. Manus (101a) was a Major General in the Austrian Service and was created Count of the Empire by Maria Theresa. He returned to Ireland where he died without male issue in 1793 and was buried in Straide Abbey. Lewis (101) was a Captain in the Austrian Service and died in 1822 aged 108 leaving four sons, three of whom died s.p., the fourth, Lewis (104) had one son, Charles (107), the senior of the line, who never married and so brought his branch of the family to a close.

Newport House Hotel

We now turn to Hugh of Newport (29) in order to continue the line. This Hugh is credited with building Newport House which today is an exclusive hotel. He married Maud Brown of Mount Brown and had eight of a family. The descent now continues through their third son, Niall (32) who renounced the Catholic faith and embraced the protestant religion, the first of the Clan to do so. It is difficult to know what prompted this action but it is believed that he was influenced by his uncle-in-law John Brown, first Lord Altamount. Niall, however, was not bigoted as he donated a free site for the Catholic Church in Newport.

In 1780 he was created Baronet. He bought the Cong Estate for a sum in excess of £20,000 and five years later purchased the Medlicot Estate, also known as Burrishoole Manor, and part of the Ormond property for £33,589-19s-4d. In addition he had land under lease from the See of Killala and a town house at 15 Merrion Square, Dublin.

This fortuitous acquisition of wealth has always been a subject of speculation. We do know he was a ship owner and it is believed he was not averse to smuggling.

He happened to hear of the whereabouts of the 'Cathach', that famous manuscript supposedly written by St. Colmcille and for centuries associated with Clann Dálaigh. It had lain for years in the safekeeping of an abbey on the Continent with the condition that only the head of Clann Dálaigh could claim it.

Sir Neal

Arming himself with a fabricated pedigree produced by the Ulster King of Arms showing him to be the 'Ó Domhnaill', he submitted a successful claim and had the relic brought back to Ireland.

He married Mary, daughter of William Coane of Ballyshannon in 1766 and had a numerous family. Of the four sons - Hugh (39a) a Colonel in the Mayo Militia and M.P.; James Moore (39b) lawyer, soldier and M.P.; Sir Neal, 2nd Baronet (39) (the first two having predeceased their father); and Connel (39c) - only Sir Neal (39) left male issue. Both Hugh and James Moore, members of Grattan's Parliament, opposed the Act of Union.

Sir Neal, 2nd Baronet married Lady Catherine, daughter of Richard, 2nd Earl of Annesley, in 1802. They had three sons. Sir Hugh, 3rd Baronet (46a) the eldest, died in 1828 leaving no male issue. The title then passed to his brother, Sir Richard Annesley (46), who was married to Mary, daughter of George Glendinning of Westport. Sir Richard had a sister, Mary, who became a Catholic and entered the Presentation Order of nuns in Galway. Sir Richard himself gave two acres of land rent-free for a Catholic school in 1852. It was he who placed the 'Cathach' in the care of the Royal Irish Academy where it remains till this day. The shrine (or cover) is on exhibition in the National Museum. Sir Richard because of financial difficulties was forced to sell off large parts of the estate. He sold 7,770 acres comprising the Cong Estate to Sir Benjamin Guinness in 1856.

Sir Richard's eldest son, Sir George (54a), 5th and last Baronet, inherited very little of the first Baronet's estate. He married a Catholic lady and, probably at her instigation, purchased and donated the site for the Convent of Mercy in Newport in 1884. He also presented the nuns with two beautiful stained glass windows. He died s.p. in 1889.

Sir Neal 2nd Bart

His brother, Richard (54), who predeceased him, had only one child, Millicent Agnes (62), therefore the male line became extinct with Sir George (54a).

However, Millicent Agnes married Edwin Thomas, who changed his name by deed-poll to

O'Donel. They had one child, George, a Lieutenant in the British Army, who was killed in action s.p. 16th June 1915.

[Source: Na Dálaigh by Rupert S. O Cochlain in Donegal Annual 1950]

N.B. Manus (29d) had a daughter, Eliza (102c) whose great grandson, Bram Stoker wrote, probably, the greatest horror story of all times – Dracula. And of course, the Dracula story is associated with Transylvania which was governed at various times by members of the Larkfield Line.

James Moore O'Donnell (39b)

Col. Hugh O'Donnell (39a)

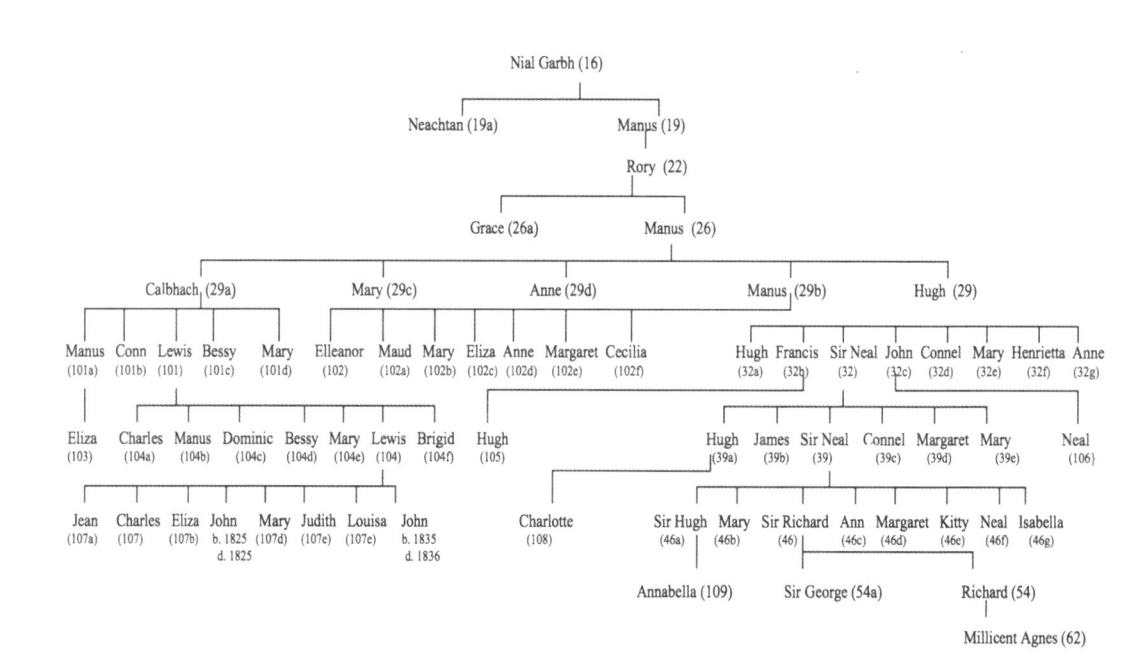

The Larkfield Line

by V. O'Donnell

Aodh Buí (17), son of Conn (7), was imprisoned along with his brother Niall Garbh (16) in 1608 but was released two years later and was given a grant of land near Rosguill in the Barony of Kilmacrennan. He died in 1649. He was married to Mary, daughter of Maguire of Fermanagh and had two sons.
Little is known of Dominic, the elder, except that he had five sons - Hugh, John, Helenus, Michael and Daniel - all of whom were mentioned in Hugh Balldearg's (23) will.
Aodh Buí's second son, John (20), was the first of the race to join the Spanish Service. He died in 1655. He married Katherine daughter of O'Rourke of Breffney and had two sons, Hugh (23) and Conall (24).

Hugh (23), the elder, was the famous "Ball Dearg".

'Ball Dearg' means a red spot about the size of a thumb-print which may be found on any part of the body but usually on the back. It is recognized as the hereditary mark of a 'true' or 'real' O'Donnell. It is often called "Ball Dearbhtha na nDálach", meaning the 'distinguishing or genuine mark of the O'Donnells'. In the Rosses area of Co. Donegal, those possessing it are said to belong to the main line of the Clan. While the 'Ball Dearg' is hereditary to the House of Larkfield, it is not uncommon among Rosses families.
Although born in Ireland, Hugh went into the Spanish Service at an early age and was known as 'Earl of Tyrconnell' abroad. At the outbreak of the Williamite Wars he desired to return to Ireland but permission was refused as England was then an ally of Spain. Balldearg, therefore, left Spain without license, reaching Cork four days after the Battle of the Boyne where he met the fleeing King James at Kinsale who recommended him to Talbot, Lord Lieutenant and Commander-in-Chief. The Irish immediately rallied to O'Donnell. This alarmed Talbot as he feared the setting up of an independent command. Talbot, allowing jealousy rather than common sense to prevail, assigned Balldearg, an experienced soldier, to the menial task of protecting the herds and followers who marched with the army. With the failure of the Jacobite cause, Balldearg found himself without either country or fortune. He was very dissatisfied with the treatment he had received since his return to Ireland. Inducements were handed out to him by Ginkel. Balldearg, realizing his position and being a professional soldier, accepted and was given a commission in the English army later to be followed by a pension. He fought in several campaigns on the Continent. On his retirement he returned to Spain where he was, apparently, pardoned. He re-entered the Spanish army and rose to the rank of Major-General. He died without issue 1703/4.

Larkfield House

His brother, Conall (24), was James II's Lord Lieutenant in Co. Donegal. He married his own cousin, Grace, daughter of Rory (22), and had two sons, Hugh (27) and Conn (27a).

Hugh (27) moved from Donegal to Mullaghbane, Co. Fermanagh, where he received a lease in excess of 31 years contrary to the Penal Laws. The land was taken from him by a Protestant 'discoverer' who had informed on him. Hugh then moved to Larkfield, Co. Leitrim where he was known as 'Earl O'Donnell' and was held in high esteem by the local Irish.

Hugh of Larkfield died in November 1754 and was buried in the Franciscan Abbey at Creevelea, Drumahair. His headstone is known locally as the 'Earl's Tombstone.' Hugh was married twice. With his first wife, Flora daughter of John Hamilton, he had three children - Conall (122), John (122a) and Susanna.

Conall (Karl in Austria) (122) went into the Austrian Service where he became Colonel Proprietor of his own regiment, to which he gave his name in 1756. He rose to the rank of General, became Inspector-General of Cavalry, a Privy Councilor and Governor of Transylvania. He was awarded the Grand Cross of the Military Order of Maria Theresa for his bravery at the Battle of Torgau, 1761. He fought in eighteen battles, was wounded several times and died in Vienna on 26th March 1771 aged 56.

John (122a) also joined the Austrian Service in 1736 and rose to the rank of Lieutenant-General. He saw much action and received the Small Cross of the Military Order of Maria Theresa at the Battle of Maxen, 1759. He later became Governor of the Elizabeth Theresian Institute, Vienna. He died on 12th March 1784 aged 72. John was married to a Kilkenny lady, Anne Carre. They had one son, Hugh, who became a Major in the Austrian Army and was killed in action at the Battle of Neerwinden in 1793. He was not married.

Hugh (27) of Larkfield's second wife was Margaret, daughter of Hugh Montgomery, Derrygonnelly, Co. Fermanagh. They had two sons - Conn (30) and John (30c).

Conn (30) of Larkfield was born in 1729. He was known as 'Ó Domhnaill' after his father died. He married Mary, sister of Sir Neal (32) of Newport 1st Baronet and had six of a family. Only two of his sons, Hugh (33) and Conn (34) were married. We now trace the line through Hugh, the elder, and later return to Conn.

Hugh (33) settled at Greyfield, Co. Roscommon and married Honora, daughter of Myles Lyons from that county. Hugh died in 1848, aged 74. He had a son, Conn (40), who married Mary Napier Phibbs, a protestant from Co. Sligo. They had one son, Constantine (47) who was six years old when his father died in 1825.

Constantine (47) was taken to England by his mother and brought up in her faith. He entered the Ministry to become a Rector of Kirkheaton, Northumberland. He married a Sligo lady and had a son, Hugh (55) born in 1861.

Hugh (55) married Anne Stafford from Morphead. He was drowned at sea in 1916 but left one son, Hugh Roe (63).

Hugh Roe (63) was born in 1897. When he was a boy he lost a leg while playing in his grandfather's sawmill at Morphead. He died s.p. in 1926 following a car accident. So ends the Greyfield Line.

We now return to Conn (34) of Larkfield.

Conn (34) 1769-1844, an artist whose portrait of O'Neill the Blind Harper hangs in the National Gallery, Dublin, remained in the old home for which he paid an annual rent of £160. He spent over £2,000 building a new house and improving the holding at Larkfield.

Despite promises, Conn failed to receive a renewal of his lease and was duly dispossessed for want of a title. He had married Mary, daughter of O'Connor Donn. Their son John (41) succeeded to Larkfield after his father's departure. Conn and his wife then went to live at Higginstown, Ballyshannon.

John (41) 1808-1874 became a Justice of the Peace and was greatly respected by the people. He is buried at Creevelea. Only one of his sons, John (48), married.

John (48) 1862-1932 was High Sheriff and Deputy Lieutenant of Co. Leitrim, a member of its first County Council and a popular local magistrate. He is interred at Dromahair. He married Brigid Ward of Manorhamilton and had a son, John (56).

John (56) was born in 1894, educated at the Holy Ghost College, Blackrock and on the Continent. He never resided at Larkfield and after the death of his father in 1932 disposed of the property. In 1945 he was recognized by Dr. MacLysaght, the Chief Herald, as 'Ó Domhnaill', Chief of Clann Dálaigh. John was married to Eileen Riedlinger of Plymouth and had three of a family. Fr. Hugh O.F.M. born 1940, who became 'Ó Domhnaill' on the death of his father in 1971 and is at present on the Zimbabwe Mission; Nuala retired and living in Co. Galway and Siobhan living in Co. Wicklow. Nuala has two of a family - Mánus and Aoife; Siobhan has four - Rónan, Rebecca, David and Conor.

Thus, Fr Hugh, if we accept the bardic traditions, is the 94th lineal descendant of Milesius of Spain who planned the Celtic invasion of Ireland more than 3,600 years ago.

Both Greyfield and Larkfield properties have been acquired and divided by the Land Commission. Larkfield House was razed to the ground about 1940 and a smaller house built on the site.

Rev. Conatantine (47)    Capt. John (Jack)(48)    John (122a)    Karl (122)

[Source: Na Dálaigh by Rupert S. O Cochlain in Donegal Annual 1950]

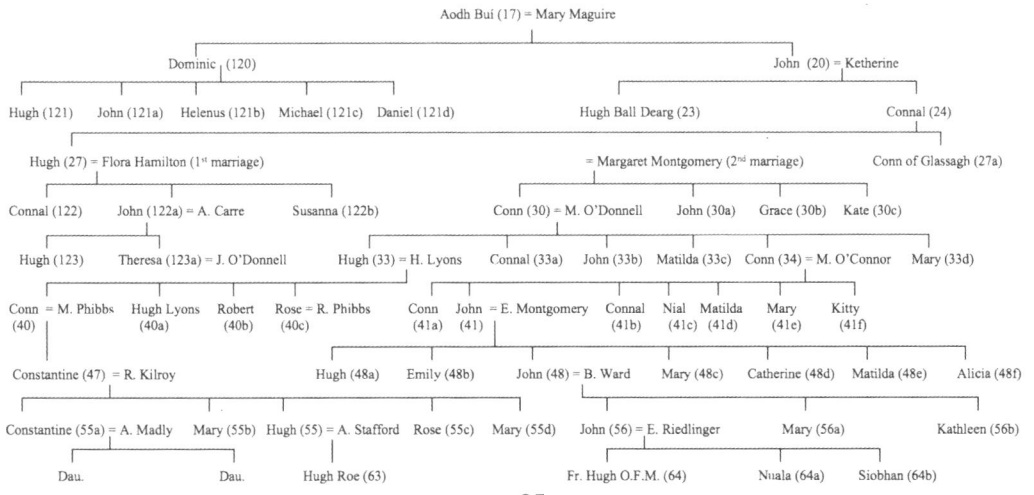

THE CASTLEBAR LINE

by V. O'Donnell

Conn Óg (18) son of Conn (7) was slain in 1601. His son Colonel Mánus (21) fought with Owen Roe O'Neill. Manus's son, Calbhach Rua (25), was a Colonel in the army of James II. He is reputed to have been the first O'Donnell to settle in Co. Mayo. He married Ellen, daughter of McSweeney Fanad, and had a son, Hugh (28), who settled in Oldcastle, Co. Mayo. Hugh married the daughter and heiress of Tirlogh O'Neill of the Fews who had been transplanted from Co. Armagh. Their son, Calbhach Dubh (31), lived first at Oldcastle and later at Aughty on the south shore of Clew Bay. Calbhach inherited the O'Neill estate but it was forfeited during the Penal Laws. This Calbhach married Mary, daughter of Colonel Manus (24) of Newport and had four famous sons - Manus (35) ancestor of the Castlebar Line, Joseph (36) ancestor of the Spanish Line, Henry (37) ancestor of the Austrian Line and Charles (38) ancestor of the Fahyness Line.

Manus (35), born 1720, was married to Elleanor Bole of Longford. Their son, Joseph (42), born circa 1751 joined his uncle in Spain, attained the rank of Captain in the Spanish Army, became involved in a duel and was obliged to return to Ireland in 1776. He then married Mary, daughter of Dominic O'Donnell of Massbrook, Co. Mayo, and had one son, Joseph (49). Later, he (42) went off to join his brother Hugh (42b) in the West Indies where he died.

Joseph Manus (49), born 1780, set out at the age of 23 to join his uncle Charles (42d) in Vienna but was detained at Hamburg and after a while sent back home. He died in 1834 and is buried at Straide Abbey. He was married to Margaret, daughter of Randal McDonald of Ballycastle, Co. Mayo, and had a son, Charles Joseph (57), born 1818.

Charles Joseph (57) was a well known barrister and Dublin Metropolitan Magistrate living in Leeson Street, Dublin. He took a keen interest in his family and collected a vast amount of genealogical material during his long life. He re-established communications with the O'Donnells of Spain and Austria which had lapsed. He supplied Dr. O'Donovan with important and original information for the Appendix to the Annals of the Four Masters. His death occurred in 1901. He married Caroline Fordatti from London

Grave of Charles Joseph (57)

and had one son, Manus Basil Hugh (65). The latter was born in 1871, became a Captain in the Royal Engineers and died unmarried in 1936, thus bringing the Castlebar line to a close. We now move to the Fahyness Line.

Charles, or Karl (38), the fourth son of Calbhach Dubh (31), was born near Swinford. In 1745 he joined his Larkfield cousins in Austria. Although he saw much action in the army, he did not advance beyond the rank of Lieutenant. As his name is dropped from the records in 1757 we assume that it was in that year he returned to Ireland. He settled in Fahyness near his birth place on an estate of 2321 acres.

Little is known about the rest of this line except the following.

His son, Hugh (45), 1750 - 1834, married Alice Jordan of Roslevin Castle, Kiltymagh in 1786 and had a son, Ignatius (53), 1783 - 1840, married Elizabeth Burke from Cork in 1810 and had a son, Edward (61), 1815 -1849, married Mary O'Brien and had a son, Ignatius (69), 1843 - 1909, married Mary Fitzgerald of Swinford in 1862 and had a son, Leopold (210), 1863 - 1865. Ignatius (69) married secondly, Mary Coughlan of Straide in 1872. They had seven of a family - Hugh Edward (72), born 1875, became a priest, went to U.S.A., died 1914; Alice (72a) died in infancy; Mary (72b) died in infancy; Joesphine (72c) died unmarried 1957; Geraldine (72d) died unmarried 1957; Evelyn (72e), a nun, died 1932; Lile (73), married Peadar O'Donnell, socialist and writer from Meenmore, Co. Donegal. Lile died s.p. in 1969. And so the Fahyness Line became extinct.

[Source: Na Dálaigh by Rupert S. O Cochlain in Donegal Annual 1950 and Rupert S. O Cochlain notes.]

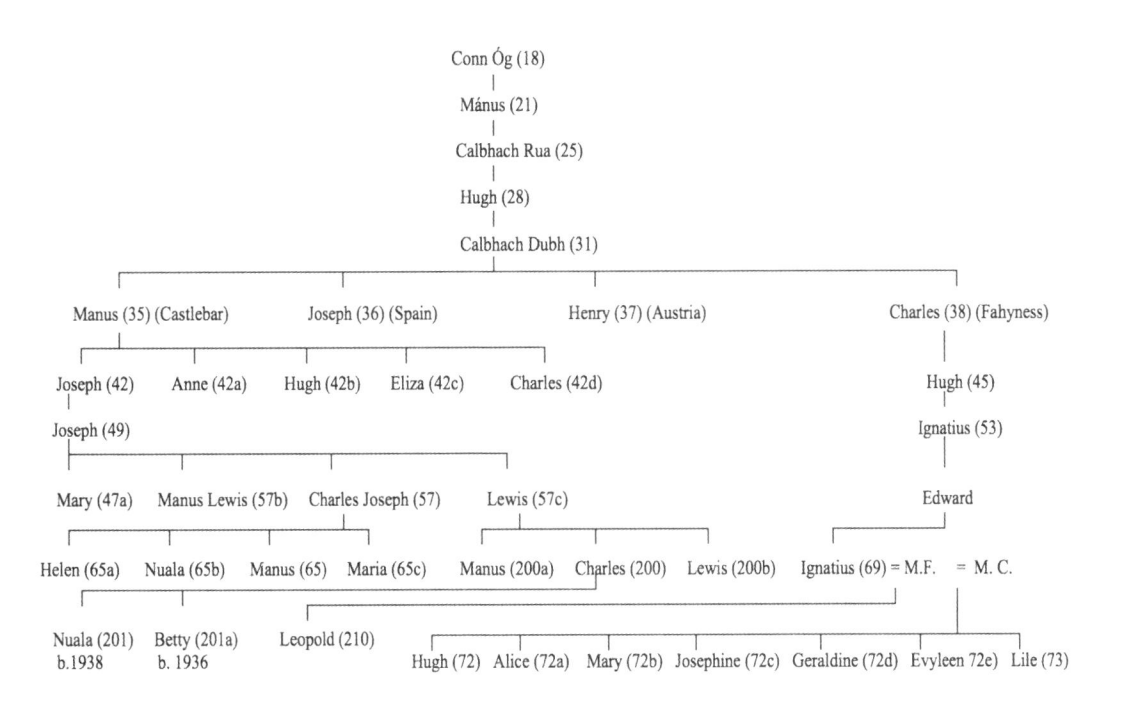

```
                              Conn Óg (18)
                                   |
                               Mánus (21)
                                   |
                           Calbhach Rua (25)
                                   |
                               Hugh (28)
                                   |
                           Calbhach Dubh (31)
    ┌──────────────────┬──────────────────┬──────────────────┐
Manus (35) (Castlebar)  Joseph (36) (Spain)  Henry (37) (Austria)   Charles (38) (Fahyness)
    │                                                                       │
┌───┬────┬────┬────┐                                                    Hugh (45)
Joseph Anne Hugh Eliza Charles                                              │
(42)  (42a) (42b) (42c) (42d)                                          Ignatius (53)
  │                                                                         │
Joseph (49)                                                              Edward
  ┌────┬──────┬──────┬──────┐
Mary  Manus Lewis  Charles Joseph  Lewis (57c)
(47a) (57b)        (57)
  ┌────┬──────┬──────┐     ┌──────┬──────┐    ┌──────┬──────┐
Helen Nuala Manus Maria  Manus Charles Lewis  Ignatius (69) = M.F.  = M. C.
(65a) (65b) (65) (65c)   (200a) (200) (200b)
  ┌─────┬──────┐
Nuala Betty  Leopold (210)
(201) (201a)        ┌──────┬──────┬──────────┬──────────┬──────────┬──────┐
b.1938 b. 1936    Hugh(72) Alice(72a) Mary(72b) Josephine(72c) Geraldine(72d) Evyleen 72e) Lile(73)
```

27

The Spanish Line

by V. O'Donnell

The O'Donnells of Spain, while ordinarily following the traditional profession of arms, found themselves at times swept along by the tide of politics and were destined to play a leading part in the affairs of the country of their adoption.

Joseph (36), born Mayo 1722, the founder of the branch, was Colonel of the Regiment of Ultonia and eventually rose to the rank of Lieutenant-General. He had a large family, four of which served in the army. They were -

Henrique (43d), born 1770 who was renowned for the part he played in the defence of the strategic town of Gerona that straddled the main highway between Barcelona and France. The defending garrison was the depleted Regiment of Ultonia consisting of 424 officers and men, under the command of Colonel Antonio O'Kelly with Major Henrique O'Donnell as second-in-command. Henrique pressed every able-bodied man into service, even forming a company of clerical students, and trained them thoroughly in the art of war. The siege lasted eighteen months and at one period an attack by 30,000 French was beaten off. He was created Count of Abisbal for reducing the Fortress of l'Abisbal at another stage in the campaign. It was here he received a leg wound that left him lame for life. He rose to the rank of Lieutenant General, became Director General of Infantry and Regent of Spain during the incapacity of Ferdinand VII. He died at Montpellier, France in 1833. His only son -Leopoldo (301), 2nd Count Abisbal and a captain of the Royal Guard was taken prisoner at Alsuzua in 1833 and shot in cold blood the next day s.p.

Alejandro (43b), born 1774, was Colonel of Infantry. He died in 1837. His only son, Jose (300), 1806-1882, was Chief of Civil Administration.

Joseph (43a), born 1772, was Knight Grand Cross of the Order of St. Ferdinand, Lieutenant General and Captain General of Old Castile and Valencia. He died in 1830 and left no male issue.

Carlos (43), born 1772/3, also had a distinguished army career. He was Captain General of Old Castile and Director General of Artillery during the Peninsular War. He died at Madrid in 1830. His son Leopoldo (51), born 1809, was the outstanding figure in Spain in his time and has been rated as one of the greatest of his race. He served in the army from an early age, winning rapid promotion. He was given the title Count de Lucena and the high post of Captain General of Cuba for his services in the Carlist War. He returned home, rose to the rank of Field Marshal, became Prime Minster and Minister of War, He conducted a brilliant campaign against the Moors that won Morocco for his country in 1860. This military victory made him tremendously popular. He was created Duke of Tetuan and received many other worthy honours in acknowledgement of his political and military skill. He died without issue in 1867 and the title went to his nephew Carlos (58). Leopoldo had three brothers, Henrique (50b), Juan (50a) and Carlos (50).

Henrique (50b), 1816-1869, was Lieutenant General and Director General of Cavalry.

Juan (50a), born 1804, Commander of the Royal Guard, was assassinated by the populace in 1836.
Carlos (50), 1802-1835, was General of Cavalry and Chief of the Royal Guard. He was killed in action. He had one son, Carlos (58).

Carlos (58), 2nd Duke of Tetuan and Marquis of Altamira, born 1834, filled many offices, among them, Minister for Foreign Affairs and Ambassador at Vienna. He kept up a close association with Ireland, corresponding with the Larkfield O'Donnells. On the occasion of the Centenary Celebrations of the death of St. Colmcille, held at Gartan on the 9th of June 1897, he sent a telegram to His Lordship, Patrick O'Donnell, Bishop of Raphoe to be read to the assemblage. The 2nd Duke died in 1903. He had two sons, Juan (66) and Leopoldo (67). The former inherited the title.

Juan (66), 3rd Duke, born 1864, became Lieutenant General of Cavalry. He, too, held many posts, among them Minister of War. Despite his lack of English, he presided over the stormy Irish Race Congress that was held in Paris in 1922. He died in 1928 leaving one son, Juan (302).

Juan (302), the 4th Juke, born 1898, died unmarried in 1932.

His sister, Blanca (303), born 1899 was the 5th to hold the title. Her house was looted during the Spanish Civil War and family records stolen or destroyed. A volume of the Annals of the Four Masters that belonged to her grandfather, the 2nd Duke, was found years afterwards in a second-hand bookshop by the Director of the Irish College, Salamanca, and restored to her. She left no children and upon her death in 1952 the title was inherited by her cousin, Leopoldo (70).

Leopoldo (70), 6th Juke of Tetuan, was born 1915. Accompanied by his wife, Consuelo, he traveled to Dublin in 1956 to be conferred with a Doctorate of Law, honoris causa, degree by the National University of Ireland. Along with his son Hugo (74), he attended the 1980 Clan Gathering in Donegal Town. He died at his residence in Madrid on the 6th October 2004, aged 89.
Hugo (74), born in 1948 is the 7th Duque de Tetuán.. He is an active member of the O'Donnell Clan Association, a Knight of Malta, a naval historian and former naval commander and Minister for the Marine. He is also a member of the Royal Academy of History (Real Academia de la Historia) in Spain. He is the next most senior O'Donnell after Fr. Hugh (64), according to the Genealogical Office, and therefore Tánaiste or heir apparent. Hugo is married to María de la Asunción Armada y Diez de Rivera and they have four of a family – Carlos Marquis of Altamira b.1974 (304) practicing law, Maria b. 1975 (305) married

to Manuel Balbás with two children, María b. 2003 and Hugo b. 2005, Hugo Marquis of Salinas b.1979 (306) is an officer of the Spanish Army and Alfonso Count of Lucena b. 1984 (307) at university.

[Source: Na Dálaigh by Rupert S. O Cochlain in Donegal Annual 1950 and family members]

Hugo (74)    Leopoldo (51)    Leopoldo (67)    Carlos (58)

Members of the Irish Race Congress which was held in Paris in 1922. It was presided over by Juan O'Donnell, Duke of Tetuan (66) from Spain seen here seated centre fron row. To his left is Eamonn De Valera and Maire Nic Suibhne (sister of Terence). To his right, Eoin Mac Neil and Sean T. O Ceallaigh. Many other famous Irish men and women were present.

Genealogical Chart No. 5   Spanish Branch

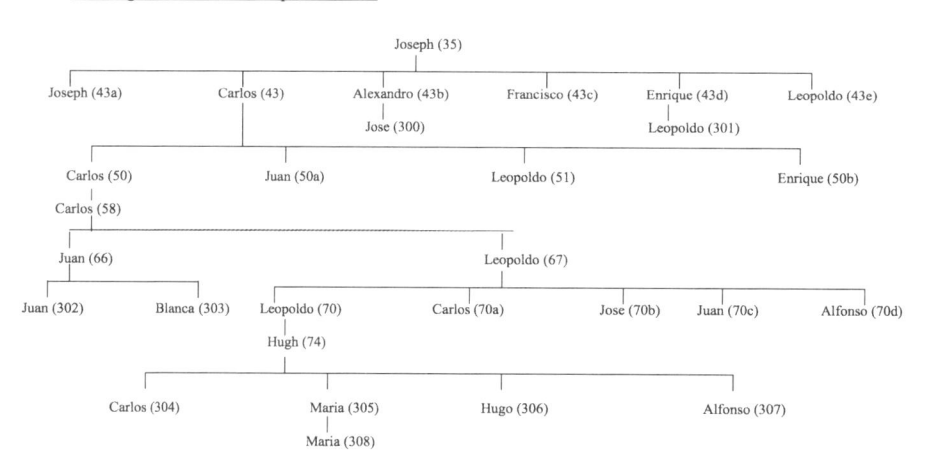

Joseph (35)

Joseph (43a)   Carlos (43)   Alexandro (43b)   Francisco (43c)   Enrique (43d)   Leopoldo (43e)
                              Jose (300)   Leopoldo (301)

Carlos (50)   Juan (50a)   Leopoldo (51)   Enrique (50b)
Carlos (58)

Juan (66)   Leopoldo (67)

Juan (302)   Blanca (303)   Leopoldo (70)   Carlos (70a)   Jose (70b)   Juan (70c)   Alfonso (70d)
                            Hugh (74)

Carlos (304)   Maria (305)   Hugo (306)   Alfonso (307)
               Maria (308)

THE AUSTRIAN LINE

by V. O'Donnell

Calbhach Dubh's (31) third son, Henry (37), born May 1726, joined his Larkfield cousins in Austria in 1742. He served in the army where on account of his courage and military skill he won rapid promotion and many rewards. 1763 found him Colonel of No. 41 Plunequette Infantry Regiment. Four years later he was in command of the O'Donnell No. 5 Cuirassiers. He retired in 1771 with the rank of Major General. Henry was over six feet tall, red haired and reputed to have been the most handsome man in the Austrian Army. He was a great favourite at Court, especially with the Empress, at whose bidding he married Leopoldine, daughter of Prince Jean Rudolf Kantacuzene. Marie Theresa gave the bride a dowry of three estates in Galicia and led her to the altar in Bratislava on her wedding day.
The title of German Count was granted to himself and his heirs by the Hapsburgs (German Emperors of the time) on account of Rory's Earl-patent granted by James I.
Major General Count Henry O'Donnell died in Galicia on 4th August 1789. He had four sons, Joseph (44), John (44a), Charles (44b), Henry (44c) and one daughter, Julie.

John (44a) 1762-1828 entered the army at an early age and achieved the rank of Major by 1804. A great student of history and art, he received an Honorary Membership of the Royal Academy of Fine Arts in Vienna. He became Imperial Chamberlain, Commander of the Royal Bavarian Max Joseph Order, and Knight of the Royal Spanish Order of Charles III. He married Caroline Countess Clari-Aldringen but left no issue.

Charles (44b) was killed, as a Major, at the storming of the Bridge of Kehl in 1796. He was unmarried.

Henry (44c) was also in the Austrian Service and died without issue.

Joseph (44), the first son of Major General Count Henry, was born in 1755. He received his early education at the Theresian Academy from which he passed to the Law School of Gottingen University. After graduating he held many important positions. He became a Privy Councillor and was made Governor of Carinthia. While serving as Minister of Finance he saved Austria from bankruptcy during the Napoleonic War. He was awarded the Grand Cross of the Order of St. Stephen for this performance.
He died suddenly in May 1810. He was married twice - firstly to Theresa, daughter of General John Count O'Donnell (122a) (Larkfield Branch) and secondly to Josephine Geisruck (sister of Cardinal Archbishop of Milan).

The first son of the first marriage was Maurice (52) born in Vienna in 1780. He had a distinguished military career, participating in many battles and retiring with the rank of Lieutenant General. He was a friend of the fabulous Madame de Stael, whose attention embarrassed him greatly. He married Christine, daughter of the Prince de Linge, a noted beauty of her day. They had two sons and two daughters. Maurice died in Dresden in 1843.

His eldest son, Maxmilian (59) 1812-1895, was the most famous of the Austrian O'Donnells. He was born in Vienna, educated in Dresden and entered the army at a young age. Having participated in engagements all over Europe he gained many awards and promotions. He had the privilege of serving as Aide-de-Camp to the Emperor, Franz Joseph I, in which capacity he saved the Emperor from assassination. In February 1853, while strolling on the bastions of Vienna, the Emperor was attacked by a man wielding a knife. Due to Max's quick action the knife only grazed the Emperor's neck. Max soon overpowered the assassin and help was summoned.

Max was showered with rewards. From the officers of the Austrian Army he received a highly ornamented and inscribed silver shield, now in the Salzburg Museum. He was conferred with the Commander's Cross of the Royal Order of Leopold and granted the status and dignity of an Austrian Count, for up till this, the title 'Count' held by the family was only by virtue of their Irish nobility. The citation continues – 'and as a further proof of Imperial and Royal grace and favour, we augment henceforth his hereditary and family arms by the insertion of our own initials and shield of our most serene ducal House of Austria; and, finally, the double-headed eagle of our Empire, to be and endured as a visible and imperishable memorial of his proved and devoted services.' This was a distinction received by only one other subject ever - Prince Schwartzenburg.

In the same citation, the surname was erroneously spelt as O'Donell. This form has been adopted by the family ever since. Friendly monarchs decorated him with orders of chivalry and the cities of Vienna, Prague, Pest, Laibach and others made him a Freeman. A magnificent Gothic Church, the Votivkirche, subscribed to by the nobility of Europe, was erected in Vienna as a mark of thanksgiving. Max was granted a site of a house on the beautiful Mirabel Platz in Salzburg. The mansion, No. 2, still stands today, the only private dwelling on this beautiful square. Alas, it is no longer in O'Donnell hands. Above the door can be seen the shield bearing the hand-held cross of the O'Donnells and the double-headed eagle of the Hapsburgs.

Max married Franziska Wagner, a marriage that was frowned upon as she was not of nobility.

Max's brother, Maurice (60) 1815-1890 served briefly in the army and was Chamberlain to the Emperor. He and his heirs were elevated to the Austrian Peerage in 1886 - which document is now the family's title of nobility. The Hapsburgs were no longer German but Austrian at this time. Maurice corresponded with Charles Joseph (57), Castlebar, and received a copy of 'The Annals of the Four Masters' when first published.

Maurice married twice, firstly to Helene, Princess Kantacuzene and secondly to Clotilde Countess Hardegg. Henry (68a) 1871-1907 was the only child from the first marriage. He entered the army and distinguished himself in the war against the Prussians in 1866. He settled in Hungary having married a Hungarian, Malwina Antonia Josepha Tornoczy-Tarnow and had two of a family, Eveline (351) and Rory (352).

Rory (352) 1871-1946, married Joanna Bauer and had one son, Henry born 1908, died s.p. in 1932 having visited Ireland once.

Eveline (351) married Nikolaus Elder von Farkas and had a son, Jenö (354) who married a Dabis Rosa. The latter had a son, Charles (355) who with his wife Edith, live in New York. They have a son, Miklos (356) and three daughters, Maria (357), Elizabeth (358) and Evelyn (359). Charles with his wife and family visited Ireland in the summer of 2004.

We now return to Maurice (60). With his second wife he had a son, Hugo (68) 1858-1904, who also served in the Austrian Army where he received several military crosses and other honours. He married Gabrille, daughter of Count von Thurn-Vallesassina-Como-Vercelli. They lived in Schloss Aigen bei Salzburg.
They had a son, Douglas (71) 1890-1970, who entered the army, fought on the Eastern Front during WW1, was taken prisoner and escaped twice. He was a fine horseman and was reputed to have been the strongest man in the Austrian Cavalry at the time.
He married Elizabeth, daughter of Count Überacker, and had four sons, all of whom served in the army during WWII. They were Mario (75a) born 1920 and died 1972; Douglas (75b) born 1921, Lieutenant with Iron Cross 1st Class, wounded and missing on the Russian Front since 1944; Johannes (76) 1926-1999, farmed on the banks of the Danube near Linz, was married to Berta Zoitel and had two children - Rory (362) living in Vienna and Maria (363) living in Steyregg near Linz. Both are unmarried.

Gabriel (75) 1922-2005, a frequent visitor to Ireland, was present at the Clan Gatherings of 1954 and '89, with his son Douglas was present in Donegal Town at a special function held to honour Rupert Coughlan in 1983. Gabriel was a farmer and business man. Being fond of animals he began, after the war, collecting and breeding animals that were on the verge extinction. Gradually the collection grew and eventually became a wild-life park and museum. Wildpark Hochkreut today is a huge attraction with thousands of visitors daily during the open season. Gabriel was married to Ulrike Leeb and had a son, Douglas (360) and a daughter, Elizabeth (361). Douglas Count O'Donell von Tyrconnell (360) is now the most senior of the Austrian Line. In Sept. 1996 he married Countess Aimeé Csáky of Hungarian descent and they have two sons, Kilian (364) and Douglas (365). The family home, which is within the Wildpark, houses many artifacts and heirlooms, among them Maxmilian's (59) glove stained with the Emperor's blood, many portraits of ancestors, patents granting titles and above all Rory's (13) patent of 1604 (sealed with the great seal of Queen Elizabeth 1 as one hadn't yet been made for King James 1) on which is outlined the peace conditions agreed upon after the defeat of Kinsale, and Maurice's (60) copy of the 'Annals' mentioned above. Douglas runs the family business today. His sister, Countess Elizabeth (361), married Andreas Hecht and they have a son, Constantine (366). Elizabeth always loved horses and has stables and a riding school.

Douglas (360) and sons

[Source: Na Dálaigh by Rupert S. O Cochlain in Donegal Annual 1950 and family members]

Genealogical Chart No. 6 The Austrian Line.

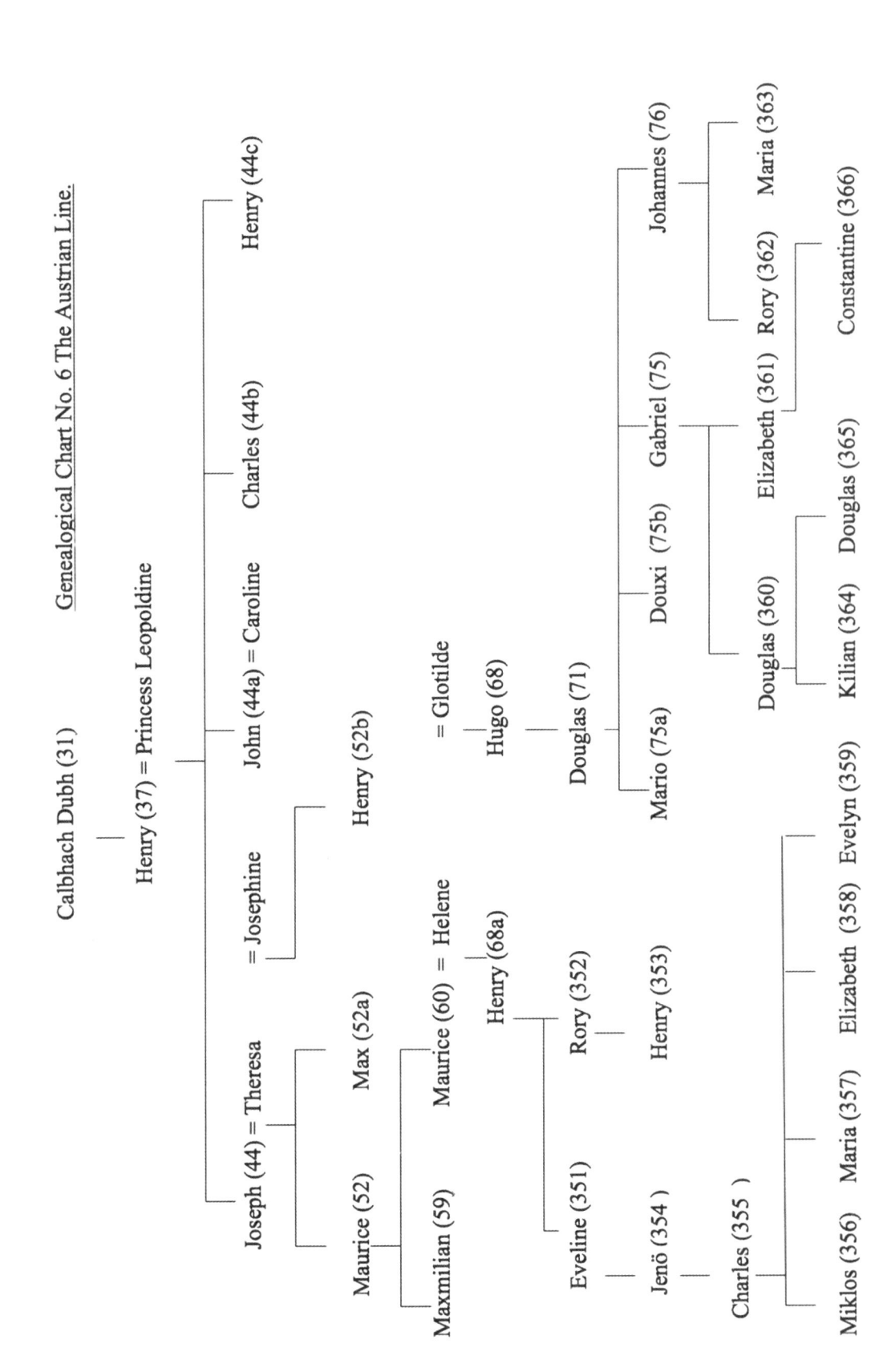

```
                                    Calbhach Dubh (31)
                                            |
                          Henry (37) = Princess Leopoldine
                                            |
        ┌───────────────────────────────────┼──────────────────────────┐
   Joseph (44) = Theresa              John (44a) = Caroline      Charles (44b)    Henry (44c)
        |                                   |
   ┌────┴────┐                        ┌─────┴─────┐
Maurice (52) Max (52a)            Henry (52b)  = Glotilde
   = Josephine                                    |
        |                                      Hugo (68)
Maurice (60) = Helene                             |
        |                                     Douglas (71)
Maxmilian (59)  Henry (68a)                       |
                    |                    ┌────────┴────────┐
                 Rory (352)          Mario (75a)      Douxi (75b)   Gabriel (75)   Johannes (76)
                    |                                                    |              |
              Henry (353)                                         ┌──────┴──────┐   ┌───┴────┐
                    |                                        Douglas (360)  Elizabeth (361) Rory (362) Maria (363)
         ┌──────────┼──────────┐                                  |
   Eveline (351)           Charles (355)                   ┌──────┼──────┬──────────┐
   Jenö (354)                                         Kilian (364) Douglas (365) Constantine (366)

   Miklos (356)  Maria (357)  Elizabeth (358)  Evelyn (359)
```

34

The O'Donnells of Glashagh

by Eunan O'Donnell

[1] Conn was a son of Connell, Lord Lieutenant 1689, and Grace O'Donnell, great-granddaughter of Sir Niall Garbh (1569-1626). As there is an absence of birth certificates for this period, we are uncertain as to whether Conn or his brother, Hugh (1691-1754) (who settled in Larkfield) was the elder. According to the family folklore, Conn was called 'Conn Spáinneach' (Conn the Spaniard), as he had travelled abroad to Spain. Perhaps, he may have been in the military service there. He returned from Spain with a considerable amount of money. He married a daughter of Gerald O'Doherty, who had lands in Ballinamore and in Dooey, Lettermacaward. Whether or not the Glashagh lands came as a dowry upon the marriage, or whether Conn bought them through his own wealth, is uncertain. What is certain is that they came into the family upon his return from Spain and his marriage. The townland gave its name to the family – the O'Donnells of Glashagh, and despite the members of the family settling in neighbouring townlands of Ballinamore, Mully, Meenmore, or further to Altnagapple in Ardara, or Aranmore Island, they still refer to their origin as Glashagh. Conn of Glashagh built a 'castle' at Glashagh. This 'castle' as it was referred to by those in the district, was a two-storey, comfortabl large farmhouse, which was larger than the neighbouring houses in the townland or the immediate district, and was therefore given the name 'castle'. Another reason for this epithet was that Conn O'Donnell had brought considerable wealth from Spain, and he enjoyed a position of eminence in the district and beyond. It was customary for the bishops and clergy of the Raphoe Diocese to gather at the O'Donnell 'Castle' in Glashagh for their annual conference. This tradition continued up until the period pre-The Great Famine, when Rory (Conn's grandson) had a disagreement with Patrick McGettigan, Bishop of Raphoe (1820-1860), over starting the Mass before the 'royalty' - the O'Donnells of Glashagh - arrived. Some of the wealth which passed through the Glashagh O'Donnells were the 'O'Donnell Pearls', which were brought from Glashagh to Aranmore Island by Anthony Rua.

[2] 'Glashagh' often written as 'Glassagh' lies in the heart of Co. Donegal, a little east of Fintown. 'na Glasaí' means 'of Glassagh.'

[3] Conn Bacach, Padaí na Glaisí, Dominic Rua & Gráinne's mother was O'Doherty, daughter of Gerald O'Doherty, Conn of Glashagh's first wife.

[4] & [5] Their mother was Timoney

[6] Mary brought the Glashagh gold plates with her to her marriage. Mary & Daniel MacDevitt owned a hotel in Glenties, County Donegal.

[7] Upon his appointment as Bishop of Raphoe in 1870, his teaching colleagues at All Hallows College, Dublin, presented him with a crozier. It is still the crozier used by the Bishop of Raphoe to this day. In 1870, the choice of bishop was between the 'Glashagh O'Donnell cousins' – Father Charles O'Donnell (1829-1885) of the Letterily O'Donnells, and his first cousin, Dr. James MacDevitt.

The Bishop's brother, Reverend John MacDevitt, was Professor of Sacred Scripture at All Hallows College, Dublin, and was the Bishop's biographer. The Bishop's other brothers, Hugh, Charles and Dan MacDevitt, Glenties, entrepreneurs and philanthropists, left their vast multi-million fortune (in today's terms) in trusts to provide for health (provision of nurses), education (educational scholarships and the provision of both the Mercy and Christian Brothers schools in Glenties – the latter never materialised, upon the direction of Bishop O'Donnell), and spiritual welfare (money for the building of Glenties and Edeninfagh churches) of the people. Another brother, Edward O'Donnell MacDevitt became Attorney General of Queensland, Australia, in 1874.

[8] P.M. Gallagher (1851-1927), born at Meentinadea, Ardara, was one of the first Catholic solicitors in south Donegal. He had a successful law practice in Donegal Town. He was a 'sterling Gael' as the inscription in the Four Masters Memorial Church states. He was the solicitor in the MacGiolla Bhrighde Irish language Law Case in 1905, with the then unknown Patrick Pearse, the later 1916 Revolutionary, as the barrister. It was Pearse's one and only law case. P.M. Gallagher had a great love of history and Gaelic culture, and with his strong O'Donnell connection, he chose a site facing the ancient Donegal Castle, as the location for his residence, Lisdanar House. It is now the site where the Post Office is in Donegal Town. P.M. Gallagher was a noted historian on the Annalists and Annals of the Four Masters. He left all his estate for the provision of a memorial to them. His trustees decided upon two memorials. An obelisk memorial in the Diamond Donegal Town, and the building of the Four Masters Memorial Church (St. Patrick's) (completed 1935).

Conn of Glashagh (died 1749/50)

son

Padaí na Glaisí (Patrick of Glashagh)

son (other children: Antoine Rua, Aranmore island, & Charles)

John[9] (came to Altnagapple in early 19th century)

son (other children: James, whose son James10 lived in Tullintain, Parish of Killaghtee, and Cornelius (Connell))

Patrick, married Sarah McNelis, sister of Bridget McNelis, grandmother of Patrick O'Donnell (1857-1927), Cardinal of Ireland.

   (other children: Charles, Bryan (b.1847), John (1834-1869), Sarah (1851-1865), Mary, Breege, Rose)

son

James (d.1887) married Mary O'Donnell11 (1839-1919), of Upper Altnagapple, Ardara.

   (other children: Connell(b.1861), Patrick (1877- 1951), James (1878-1904), Michael (1885-1961), Mary (b.1861), Bridget (1883-1938), Ann (1877-1946))

son

Johnny (1874-1943) married Ann Kenny, Altnagapple Upper.

   (other children: Michael (d. 1971), Mary Ann (d. 1989), also twin girls who died in infancy)

son

John F. (1911-1980) married Annie Carr (1917-1993), Largybrack, Ardara.

   (other children: Mary Agnes (b.1940), Bridget Christina (b.1943), Nancy (b.1950), Noreen (b.1955))

son

Edward John (b.1938) married Mary Harvey (b.1940), Drimnaherk East, Parish of Inver.

   (other children: Maria Marcella (Moya) (b.1968), Annette Regina (b.1969), Orla Noelle (b.1972)

son

Eunan (b. 1974) author of this article

[9] The O'Donnells of Altnapple have kept the O'Donnell of Glashagh names – John, Connell (Conn), Patrick, James, and Charles. These are names familiar to the Larkfield, Austrian and

Spanish O'Donnells. Juan (John) and Carlos (Charles) are familiar among the Spanish O'Donnells. Like the O'Donnells of Glashagh, many of the O'Donnells of Altnagapple had red hair, and bore the epithet 'Rua'/ 'Ruadh', which means 'Red haired'.

[10] James' son, Joseph (1868-1919), a National School teacher in Dunfanaghy, left for South Africa; while there he joined the Kitchener Fighting Scouts in the Boer War (1899-1902), and was promoted to the rank of Sergeant Major, for distinguished service and leadership at Spits Kop and Modder Spruit in the Transvaal. He wrote a 21 page letter home to his mother, Isabella, in which he professed his love for South Africa, and that he was 'as happy as a prince' (original letter [28th August 1901] in the possession of Edward & Mary O'Donnell, Riverside House, Ardara)

[11] Mary O'Donnell of Upper Altnagapple's first cousin, Neil O'Donnell emigrated from Upper Altnagapple in the last quarter of the 19th century. He and his wife, Mary settled in Kokomo, Indiana. Neil's son, Father Charles Leo O'Donnell (1885-1934), became President of the University of Notre Dame, Indiana (1928-34).

[12] The O'Donnells of Aranmore the present day, are not the same O'Donnells as the 'O'Donnells of the Pearls'. The male line is extinct in this Aranmore O'Donnell branch. The O'Donnell Pearls should now pass to the nearest male line, the O'Donnells of Altnagapple.

[13] Antoine Rua arrived in Aranmore Island in the early 19th century. According to the folklore of the area, it is said that he wore his hair long in the manner of a 17th century prince. He brought the 'O'Donnell Pearls' from Glashagh to Aranmore.

[14] Mary was the second eldest of this family. She married Andrew Aiken on 16th July, 1908, but separated within a year, due to the unhappiness of the marriage. Andrew had been previously married to Hannah Coll of Aranmore (m. 7th May 1904). Hannah Coll died 9th December 1907. He had one child by this marriage to Hannah Coll. There were no children by the Aiken-O'Donnell marriage. Mary Aiken (née O'Donnell) went to work in Scotland & London. On her return for her mother's death in 1918, she brought the O'Donnell Pearls, a family heirloom from Glashagh, back to her home in the UK. She met Mr. Ernest A. Chapman, a London hairdresser, who became her partner, and he published several pamphlets describing the famous pearls. In 1958, the Duke of Tetuan went to see them in their place of safekeeping in the Bank of England vaults.

[15] Of whom the praise poem 'Dominic Ruadh na Glaisighe' was written by Máire Chonnachtach. See: MacMeanmain, Seaghán, Old John (1937). He was a highly cultured and learned man in Latin. He was noted for his hospitality. The O'Donnells of Glashagh were the only lay people in the district who spoke Latin at this period. They had Spanish wines imported in Killybegs for their household. They were educated in Spain, and corresponded with the Spanish O'Donnells.

[16] Brigid met her future husband at a pilgrimage to Gartan, where the family's patron saint, St. Colmcille was born. Manus O'Donnell travelled on a steed, and wore a sword when he visited Glashagh to ask for Brigid's hand in marriage from her father, Dominic Rua. Dominic required that the request be written out in Latin. Manus, having been educated in Latin, had no difficulty in adhering to Dominic's request. He was allowed to marry Brigid.

[17] Rory was secretary to the Catholic Emancipation Committee in Stranorlar. He was also on the Grand Jury at Lifford. When the Great Famine (1845-1847) occurred, he had Brian Quinn slaughter the O'Donnell cattle to feed the multitude of poor and hungry in the locality. The O'Donnells of Glashagh held the etiquette that the Mass was not to start before

they arrived. On this one particular occasion, they arrived at the scálan (make shift chapel which was a carry over from Penal Days when no proper chapel buildings were allowed) , having been delayed themselves by a flood in the River Finn, to discover that the priest had started the Mass without them. Rory, leading the O'Donnells of Glashagh entered, and when the priest had finished the prayer, Rory said angrily: "How bold it is of you to start the Mass without our arrival". The priest replied that the congregation were wet to the skin, and hence the start. Rory retorted with aristocratic displeasure: "I am Rory, son of Dominic Rua, son of Conn, of the fifth generation removed from omnipotent princes". The little priest who had his back turned to the congregation up until this point, removed his large coat, and turned to face them. To their surprise it was the bishop himself, Bishop McGettigan. He faced Rory, and said: "O'Donnells, understand this, that I am Patrick, son of Conall, son of Thomas McGettigan, of the second and third generation removed from Fanad fishermen!" An argument ensued in Latin between the two men.

[18] Mary was the last of the O'Donnells of Glashagh line to be educated in Spain.
[19] Either Roger or his brother Dominick was a military cadet in Spain.
[20] Two sisters, Margaret and Ann 'Rory' O'Donnell, married their first cousins, the brothers Padaí & Eoin na Glaisí, son of Dominic Rua.
[21] Teague & John emigrated to New Zealand circa 1900.

Donegal Castle 1961 – John F. O'Donnell (1911 -1980), Altnagapple, Ardara, (whose great-great-grandfather, John O'Donnell, came from Glashagh), his wife, Annie (1917-1993), and their neighbour, Mrs. Mary Diver.

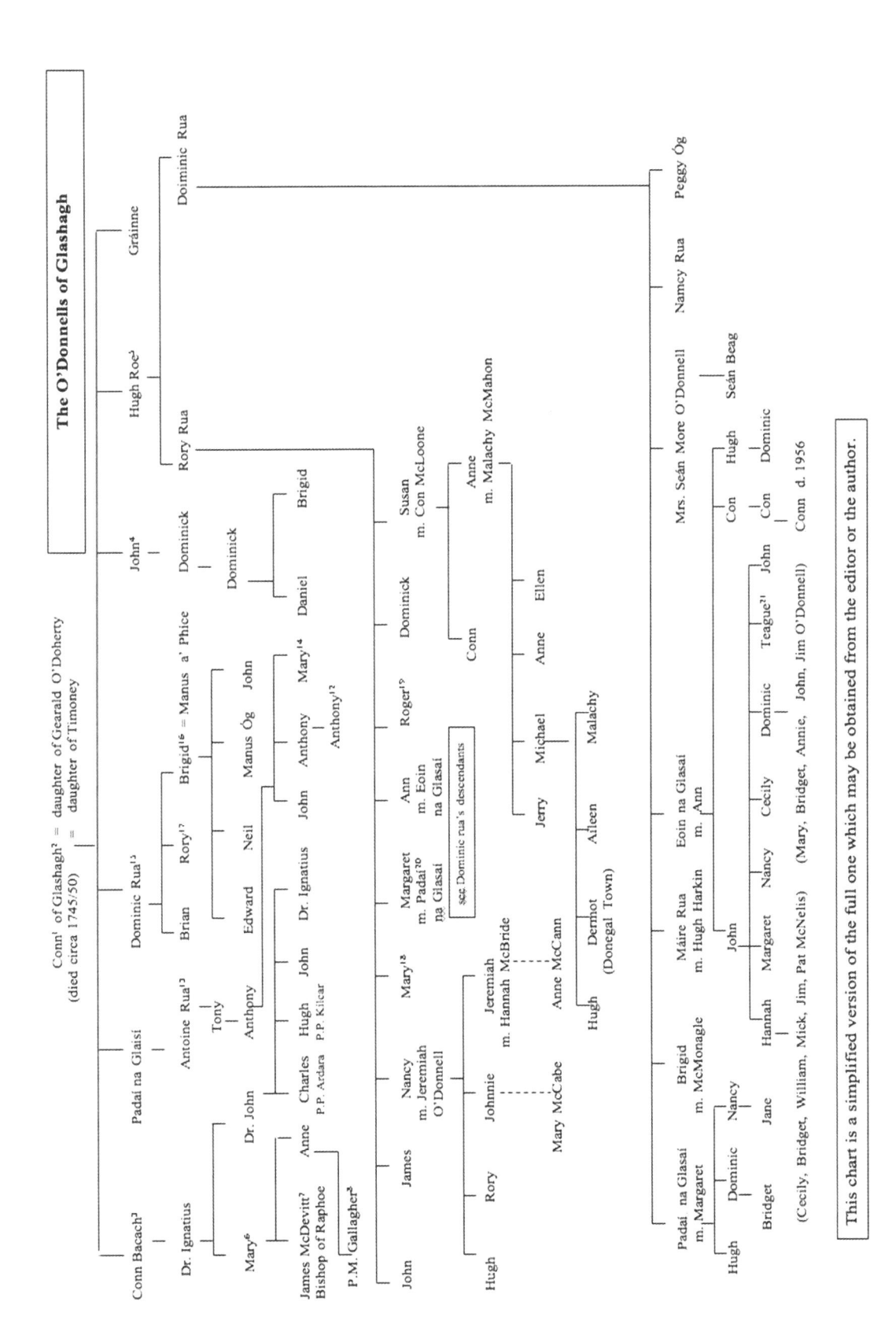

The O'Donnells of Glashagh

Conn[1] of Glashagh[2] = daughter of Gearald O'Doherty
(died circa 1745/50) = daughter of Timoney

- Conn Bacach[2]
  - Dr. Ignatius
  - Mary[6]
    - James McDevitt[7] Bishop of Raphoe
    - Anne
      - P.M. Gallagher[8]
      - John
        - James
          - Hugh
            - Rory
            - Johnnie
              - Jeremiah m. Hannah McBride
              - Mary McCabe ---- Anne McCann
                - Hugh
                  - Dermot (Donegal Town)
                    - Aileen

- Padaí na Glaisí
  - Dr. John
    - Charles P.P. Ardara
    - Hugh P.P. Kilcar
    - John
    - Dr. Ignatius
  - Antoine Rua[13]
    - Anthony
      - Tony
  - Dominic Rua[13]
    - Brian
      - Edward
    - Rory[17]
      - Neil
    - Brigid[16] = Manus a' Phice
      - Manus Óg
      - John
      - Anthony[12]
        - Anthony
    - Mary[14]
      - John
  - Mary[18]
    - Nancy m. Jeremiah O'Donnell
    - Margaret m. Padaí[20] na Glasaí
      see Dominic rua's descendants
  - Daniel
    - Dominick
    - Roger[19]
      - Jerry
      - Michael
        - Malachy

- John[4]
  - Dominick
    - Dominick
    - Brigid
  - Susan m. Con McLoone
    - Anne m. Malachy McMahon
      - Conn
      - Anne
      - Ellen
  - Ann m. Eoin na Glasaí

- Hugh Roe[5]

- Gráinne
  - Doiminic Rua

- Rory Rua
  - Peggy Óg
    - Padaí na Glasaí m. Margaret
      - Hugh
        - Bridget
      - Dominic
        - Jane
      - Nancy
      - Brigid m. McMonagle
        - Hannah
      - Máire Rua m. Hugh Harkin
        - John
        - Margaret
      - Eoin na Glasaí m. Ann
        - Nancy
        - Cecily
        - Dominic
        - Teague[21]
        - John
    - Nancy Rua
    - Mrs. Seán More O'Donnell
      - Con — Con
      - Hugh
      - Dominic
    - Seán Beag

(Cecily, Bridget, William, Mick, Jim, Pat McNelis)   (Mary, Bridget, Annie, John, Jim O'Donnell)   Conn d. 1956

This chart is a simplified version of the full one which may be obtained from the editor or the author.

The Ramelton Line

by V. O'Donnell

Returning to Aodh Óg Dubh (3) who was a brother of Mánus 21st Chieftain, we find he was married to Máire, daughter of O'Rourke, Lord of Leitrim and seems to have had two other wives as well, the last being a daughter of O'Connor, Sligo with whom he had two sons Calbhach (408) and Neachtain (409). Both are mentioned in the O'Clery Genealogies. Calbhach had a son, Aodh Buí (413), who was Colonel in the Irish Army 1641-49. There is a poem addressed to him in the 'Book of O'Donnell's Daughter' which is now in Brussels (MS Brussels 6131-3).

With his second wife, Aodh Óg Dubh had four sons - Mánus Óg (404), Tarlach (405), (both of these are mentioned in the inquisition of 1626), Eineachan (406) and Seán (407).

With his first wife, Aodh (3) had one son, Cathbharr (401) living in 1615 and married to Elizabeth, daughter of Conn (7), son of Calbhach Chief (4). Aodh Dubh Óg (or Aodh Óg Dubh) died in 1618.

Cathbharr (401) had two sons, Col. Tarlach (402), a leader of 1641 and Commander of the O'Donnell Regiment who fought against Cromwell, and Neachtain (403) who was wounded fighting at Glenmaquin 1642.

Col. Tarlach was married to Joan, daughter of Tarlach O'Donnell of Cúl Mhic an Tréan (Castleforward) and had several sons and a daughter, Mary, who married Edmund O'Malley of Bealclare, Co. Mayo. The first son was Conn (410) who succeeded his father as Commander of the Regiment and was killed in action at Wexford.

The second son of Col. Tarlach was Brigadier Daniel O'Donnell (411), 1665-1738. He fought at the Boyne and later took his regiment with him to France where he spent his fortune bringing other O'Donnells to the Continent to replenish the Regiment.

It was Brig. O'Donnell who brought the 'Cathach' to the Continent. On seeing the erosion of the old Gaelic System at the hand of the Sassanach who destroyed everything Irish or Catholic, Daniel feared that the 'Cathach' would suffer the same fate as other Gaelic relics. Before his final departure, he took (without permission) the 'Cathach' from its place of safekeeping in the little church of Ballymagroarty and brought it with him to the Continent. He deposited it in a Monastery in Belgium with the condition that only the head of Clann Dálaigh could reclaim it.

Brig. O'Donnell married Theresa, daughter of Robert Strickland of Catterick, Yorkshire, and widow of John Stafford, controller of the King's Household at St. Germain. They had a daughter who was 14 years of age in 1735. Nothing further is known of this family.

[Source: Na Dálaigh by Rupert S. O Cochlain in Donegal Annual 1950]

Genealogical Chart No. 7   Ramelton Line.

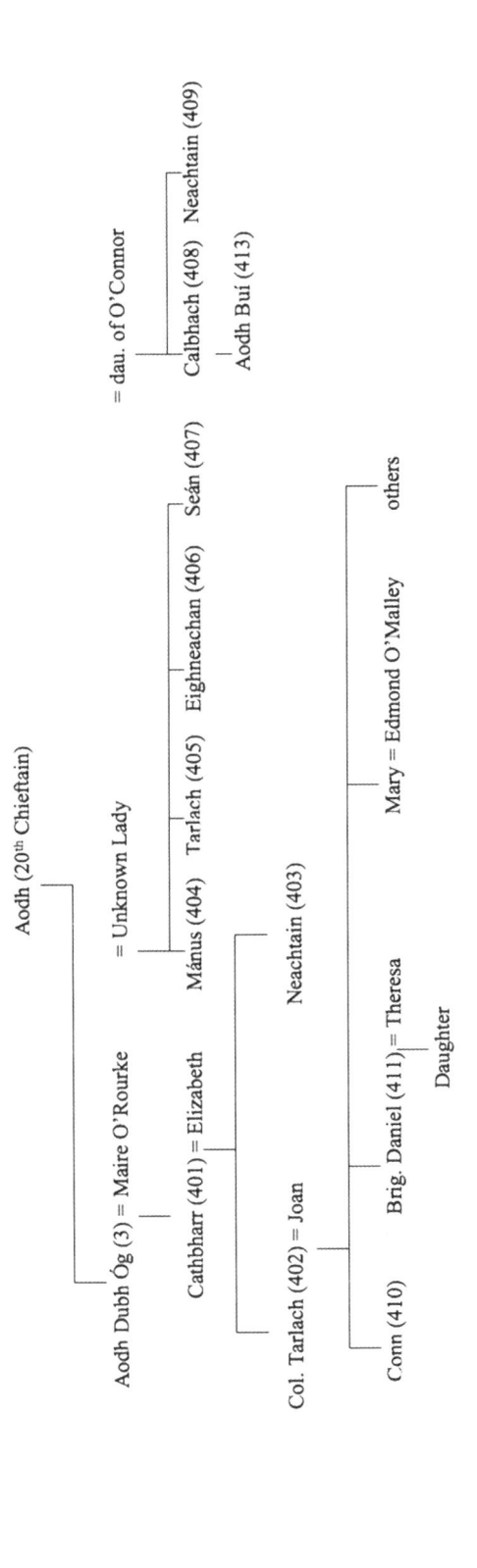

Aodh (20th Chieftain)

Aodh Dubh Óg (3) = Maire O'Rourke   = Unknown Lady   = dau. of O'Connor

Cathbharr (401) = Elizabeth   Mánus (404)   Tarlach (405)   Eighneachan (406)   Seán (407)   Calbhach (408)   Neachtain (409)

Neachtain (403)   Aodh Buí (413)

Col. Tarlach (402) = Joan

Conn (410)   Brig. Daniel (411) = Theresa   Mary = Edmond O'Malley   others

                Daughter

41

The Rosses O' Donnells

by V. O'Donnell

Donnchadh Scaite

Looking at the first genealogical chart we see a question mark at (8) the first son of Aodh Dubh (5). His name does not appear in historical records - they merely indicate that the first-born of the first marriage was a son and the English expressed a certain concern over his birth as they expected him to inherit his father's title. Aodh Dubh had submitted to the English and therefore had to accept an English title. English titles were hereditary unlike those of the Irish. There were several more sons by this marriage but they didn't live long enough to present any problem. Aodh Dubh, after the death of his first wife, remarried. His second wife was 'Ineen Dubh.' Their first-born was a son - the famous Aodh Rua (12). As Aodh grew up, his mother, a very ambitious woman, was determined that nothing should stand in the way of her darling Red Hugh becoming the next 'Ó Domhnaill.' It is said she had the sword arm of the first son of the first marriage disabled thus eliminating him from election to the high office.

Tradition says that his name was Donnchadh (Dennis) and after the above incident his father appointed him steward of the Rosses where he was ever after known as 'Donnchadh Scaite.' His descendants are said, to be numerous in the Rosses and surrounding areas till this day.

Seán Mac Mánus Óg

Aodh Dubh (5) had a brother, Mánus Óg (6) whose son, Seán had land in Inishown. It seems this Seán took no active part in the Nine Years War, but after the Flight of the Earls the English moved into Ulster and it became quite apparent that there was going to be no recognition of Sean's good behavior. In 1608 Seán and Cahir O'Doherty were forced to make a last stand to defend their homes, but outnumbered, their struggle was a short one. O'Doherty was killed leaving Seán in command. When it became clear that the situation was hopeless, Seán retreated to Tory Island where he had a fort. But it wasn't long until he had to leave Tory. It is told that his departure from Tory was so hasty that he left his wife and family behind, and as his boat pulled away from the island under cover of darkness he came within oar's length of the English boats approaching the island but seemingly the English were too preoccupied with their landing to notice the fleeing Seán.

Seán's next refuge was on Aranmore Island but not for long. From here he fled to the Rosses where the English failed to find him. No more appears in the records but tradition has it that Seán Rua Ó Domhnaill fled from the Braes of Derry after 'Cogadh na hÉireann' and settled on Inis Saile, a little Rosses island not far from Burtonport. We have every reason to believe that Seán Rua of Inis Saile was Seán Mac Mánus Óg. His descendants, like those of Donnchadh Scaite, are numerous in that part of the County.

It was customary for the O'Donnells of Inis Saile to name their first son Seán after their ancestor. Here is a list of those Seáns from Seán Rua down - Seán Dearg, Seán Garbh, Seán Giortach, Seán Leathan, Seán Beag, Seán Mór, Seán Bheagaide and Johnnie. Johnnie had no family but his brother Donnchadh who was born in 1858 had a son, Seán who was a guard in Sligo. Seán's first son was born on St. Patrick's Day and was christened 'Pádraig' thus ending the custom.

Many of Seán's descendants had the 'Ball Dearg' and they claimed to be 'na Dálaigh Chearta' the true O'Donnells.

Newport Graves

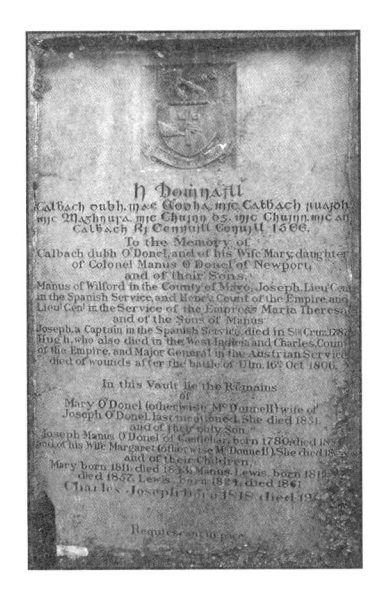

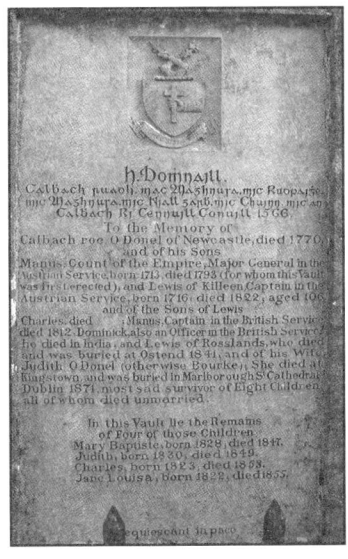

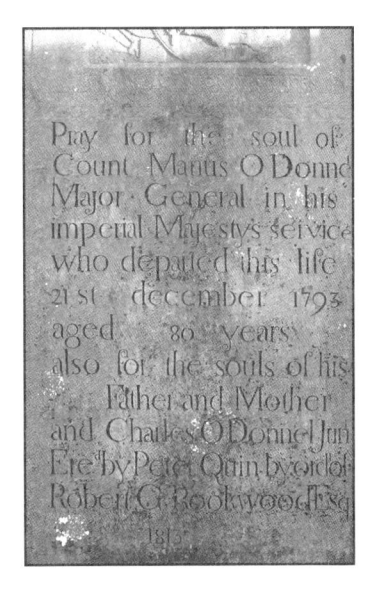

Memorials attached to the O'Donnell vault at Straide Abbey, Co. Mayo

Inauguration of a Chieftain

by Rupert S. Ó Cochláin

Doon Rock

The selection of a Chieftain was with the permission and by the advice of the nobles, both lay and ecclesiastical of the Clan. Those eligible for the high office were required to be of the blood of the original conqueror or acquirer of the territory. Selection was confined to the 'Dearbhfine' - a specified family group spanning four generations. Other requirements were that the successful candidate should be free from blemish and of a fit age to lead his people in the field.

The inauguration ceremony had both its religious and civil sides. The former was conducted by the successor of St. Colm Cille viz. the Bishop of Derry and the coarb of Kilmacrennan, in the nearby Abbey. The presence of O'Friel, the coarb concerned, was indispensable as he was the actual Inaugurator.

The civil ceremony took place on the rock of Doon in the presence of the Clan. The ruler-elect removed his footwear and stood in the imprint of the feet of the first Chieftain that was cut into the Inauguration Stone. O'Clery, the Ollamh, came forward and read aloud a brief summary of the laws and customs in accordance with which the Clan should be governed. An oath was then administered that these ancient practices would be preserved inviolate.
This done, the candidate set aside his sword and was presented with 'An Slat Bhan', a straight white rod, as an emblem of purity and rectitude and a reminder that his judgment should be unbiased and that he should be pure and upright in his actions. It was also an indication that his people would be obedient to him and that no other weapon would be required to command them. A sub-Chief next replaced one of the wearer's sandals as a token of submission and threw the other over his shoulder for luck.
Then, 'amid the clang of bucklers, music of harps and cheers of the whole assembly,' the Chieftain was proclaimed by the Inaugurator who, in a loud voice, pronounced the surname 'O'Domhnaill' only, which was taken up by the Clergy, sub-chiefs, Freeholders and finally by the whole gathering.

Having been thus inaugurated the new Chieftain stepped down from the stone and turned around thrice forwards and thrice backwards (in honour of the Holy Trinity) to view his territories and show himself to his people.
(The ornamented Inauguration stone was kept in Kilmacrennan Abbey, where it survived until c. 1775 when it was smashed to smithereens by an anti-Irish bigot).

An Cathach

by V. O'Donnell

The Cathach, a Latin version of the Hebrew Psalms of the Old Testament, has the distinction of being both Ireland's oldest ecclesiastical manuscript and the earliest example of Irish writing. The penmanship is attributed to St. Colmcille who according to tradition copied it from the original belonging to his old teacher, St. Finnian of Maigh Bhille. Finnian, on hearing about the copy, demanded its surrender but Colmcille refused. To resolve the matter, it was decided to bring it before the High King, Diarmad Mac Cearbhaill, for judgment. 'Colmcille transcribed my book without my knowledge," charged Finnian, "and I maintain that the transcript belongs to me.'
'I hold,' countered Colmcille, 'that Finnian's book has not decreased in value because of the transcript I made from it, and that it is not right to extinguish the divine things it contained, or to prevent me, or anybody else, from copying it, or reading it or from circulating it through the provinces. I further maintain that if I have benefited from its transcription, which I desire to be for the general good, provided no injury accrues to Finnian, or his book, thereby it is quite permissible for me to copy it.'
Copyright was not yet covered under the Brehon Law (it is very likely that this was the very first case of such anywhere). After much thought, the High King declared: 'Le gach bóin a bóinín agus le gach leabhar a macleabhar.' (To every cow belongs her calf and to every book belongs its copy). Therefore he found for Finnian. Colmcille was greatly angered by this decision and being of noble birth, rallied the northern forces, met and utterly defeated the High King's army at Cúl Dréimre, Co. Sligo A.D. 561.
Public opinion and remorse at the slaughter caused by his selfishness caused Colmcille to go into exile. He promised to win as many souls for Christ as were killed in the battle.
We are not sure how much truth there is in this tradition but we are sure the Cathach did exist and remained in Donegal in the possession of Colmcille's own kinsmen, the O'Donnells. Cathbharr (died 1106) the first of the race to assume the surname, 'Ó Domhnaill,' commissioned Domhnall Mac Rabhartaigh to make a shrine for the relic.
In time the Cathach became a cherished relic of the O'Donnells. It played an important part in the inauguration ceremony of a chieftain.

> 'Here he swore upon the Cathach,
> Held aloft the willow wand
> While ten thousand tribesmen hailed him
> And awaited his command.'

In the Gaeltacht areas of Donegal, one can still hear a person swear, 'Dar a leabhra!' (By the book).

But the Cathach, is probably, best known for its use in time of battle. The following quotation is from 'Beatha Cholmcille' written by Manus O'Donnell (2) in the sixteenth century – 'The Cathach indeed is the name of the book on account of which battle was fought. It is

Colmcille's chief relic in the land of Cinel Conaill Gulban. It is encased in gilded silver, and it is not lawful to open it. And if it be taken thrice right-hand wise round the host of Cinel Conaill when about to engage in battle, they always return safe in triumph. It is on the bosom of a comharb or a cleric who is as far as possible free from mortal sin that it should be borne round the host.'

The MacRoartys became the hereditary custodians of the Cathach and had it kept in the little Columban church of Ballymagroarty beside Ballintra. Nothing of the church remains today.

According to the Annals of the Four Masters the Cathach once fell into enemy hands when in 1497 Conn O'Donnell was defeated by MacDermot of Moylurg. MacRoarty was slain and the holy relic taken. Clann Chonaill, two years later, under the Chieftaincy of Red Hugh O'Donnell, marched against MacDermot, defeated him and recovered the Cathach.

It was undoubtedly brought to Kinsale on that wintry journey of 1601. Was the sacred ceremony of bearing it in the prescribed manner thrice around the forces of Tyrconnell, on that terrible night of lightening and St. Elmo's fire, before setting out from the Irish camp for the pre-dawn attack on the English observed? Did MacRoarty, bearing the sacred relic, march with O'Donnell? Where was it during the ensuing melee, and how did it escape destruction or capture?

And why did Rory (13) not bring it with him on the 'Flight' of 1607?

On seeing the collapse of the old Gaelic system, confiscation of property and the general chaos that followed the 'Flight,' Brig. Daniel O'Donnell (411), after the Treaty of Limerick, brought it with him to the Continent. He had a silver case made for it in 1723 as its condition had suffered much down the years. Later he had it deposited in a monastery with certain conditions for its retrieval. Indeed much credit is due to Brig. Daniel for providing the safekeeping of the relic during his lifetime as otherwise it might easily have been lost forever.

More that three quarters of a century was to pass before the Cathach came to light again. Upon its discovery on the Continent, Sir Neal O'Donel of Newport (32) had a false pedigree drawn up by the Deputy King of Arms for a fee of one thousand pounds declaring him head of Clann Dálaigh. With this document he claimed the Cathach. His claim was successful and the sacred relic soon found a new resting place in Newport House, Co. Mayo.

But while Sir Neal held the relic he was not aware of its contents but believed it to be bones. It was not until after his death in 1811, when formally opened by Sir William Betham, that it was discovered to house a manuscript. Here is a description of what was found.

'The contents were found to be a rude wooden box, very much decayed, enclosing a manuscript on vellum, a copy of the ancient vulgate translation of the psalms, in Latin, of fifty-eight membranes. It appeared to have been originally stitched together, but the sewing had almost entirely disappeared. On one side was a thin piece of board, covered with red leather, very like that with which eastern manuscripts are bound. It was so much injured by damp as to appear almost a solid mass; by steeping it in cold water I was enabled to separate the membranes from each other, and by pressing each separately between blotting paper, and frequently renewing the operation, at length succeeded in restoring, what was not actually decayed, to a legible state.'

Sir Richard (46), grandson of Sir Neal, deposited the Cathach in the Royal Irish Academy for safe-keeping for the people of Ireland in 1843. The shrine is now on display in the National Museum, Dublin while the manuscript reposes in the R.I.A. library.

In 1920 the manuscript was sent to the British Museum for restoration. Each leaf was inserted in a frame of strong paper, a recognized method of preserving fragile material, and the whole expertly rebound.

In 1980 further repair and rebinding work was carried out. This work was by Roger Powell (who had rebound the Book of Kells), at a cost of eight thousand pounds sterling. The paper mounting from which the vellum leaves had come adrift was replaced with new vellum mounts specially stained to match the colour of the original leaves. Pieces of degreased fish skin were used for joining the butted edges in the vellum mounts. The leaves were then bound in English oak boards. A box was specially designed to keep the vellum under pressure in order to prevent 'cockling.'

A booklet entitled, 'The Cathach of Colum Cille' by Michael Herity and Aidan Breen was published by the Royal Irish Academy in 2002. It is a beautiful publication with a CD ROM of all images. See www.ria.ie ISBN 1-874045-92-5

The Cathach with box and lid and explanatory booklet. Photo by V. O'Donnell with kind permission of the R. I. A.

The Capture and Escape of Red Hugh

by V. O'Donnell

The opening lines of 'Beatha Aodha Ruaidh Uí Dhomhnaill' written by Lughaidh O'Cléirigh in 1616 and translated by Rev. Dennis Murphy in 1893 are as follows, 'A famous progency sprung from O'Donnell.' (The O'Donnell referred to being Aodh Dubh (5)). Ineen Dubh, daughter of James MacDonnell, Lord of the Isles (of Scotland) was wife of that same O'Donnell and mother of the most renowned of his children - Aodh Rua (the 'progency'), Rory, Manus and Caffir. Having been fostered by several of the noble houses of Ulster, 'then he continued to grow and increase in comeliness and urbanity, tact and eloquence, wisdom and knowledge, goodly size and noble deeds, so that his name and fame spread throughout the five provinces of Erin among the English and the Irish, even before he passed the age of boyhood and completed his fifteenth year.'

It seems that the birth of Aodh fulfilled many prophecies including one by St. Colmcille - 'there will come a man glorious, pure, exalted, who will cause mournful weeping in every territory; he will be the god-like prince, and he will be king for nine years.' All this, plus the fact that Aodh's sister, Joan, was betrothed to Aodh O'Neill disturbed the English to such an extent that they planned to imprison him from an early age.

The kidnapping of Aodh Rua is a famous story and subject of the Irish poem,'Fuadach Aodh Rua.' In September 1587, the Lord Deputy, Sir John Perrot, sent a ship disguised as a Spanish merchantman to Rathmullan where she dropped anchor opposite the castle of MacSweeney, where Aodh Rua was visiting at the time. Aodh, along with some of his friends, was invited aboard to sample the fine wines and beers brought by the ship. The youths, unsuspectingly, accepted. While they were enjoying 'Spanish hospitality' they were suddenly seized, unarmed and imprisoned in a well-secured apartment, while the crew on deck weighed anchor and prepared to sail. As the ship reached deep water, those on shore realised what was happening but by then it was too late to take action.

On arrival in Dublin Aodh was incarcerated in the Castle. During his stay there he never gave up seeking a means to escape. This of course was difficult as the tower (probably the Birmingham Tower) in which he was kept was a tall, strong structure surrounded by deep water and, of course, well guarded. However, with the aid of outsiders, a plan was formed. Towards the end of December 1590 a rope was smuggled into his cell. On a pre-arranged night Aodh, along with his cell mates managed to remove the iron bars from the window. They then lowered themselves by means of the rope to the ground outside the tower. The guard on the main gate, it seems, was well bribed to neglect his duty for a brief moment that night.
Outside the walls a guide (Art Kavanagh was his name) was waiting who quickly led them from the city.
But the boys, wearing bad footwear and through lack of strength and exercise, soon grew tired. The guide was sent for help to Phelim O'Toole, whom the youths regarded as a friend. However, to their great disappointment, they were soon handed back to the English and this

time their confinement was more severe. Aodh was bound in chains and the guard doubled. But he was determined to escape. A second plan began to take shape and about a year later, on the fifth of January, 1592 (**oidhche nottlacc stell** = eve of Christmas of the Star = eve of the Epiphany) Aodh made his second attempt. His comrades on this occasion were Henry and Art O'Neill, sons of Shane the Proud, with whom he had shared his cell since his recapture. Files had been smuggled in (it is believed that Aodh O'Neill had much to do with the business) with which they cut their bounds, and again, they descended by rope, crossed the moat and with the help of a guide made their way out of the city. The weather on this occasion was more inclement than on the previous attempt and in their haste they lost Henry O'Neill. As they left the city behind and began to climb the Wicklow Hills the rain turned to sleet and snow from which they suffered being poorly clothed. Soon Art became exhausted and had to be helped along by Aodh and the guide but after a while the going became impossible. At this stage Aodh and Art sought the shelter of a lofty cliff while their guide proceeded to Fiach Mac Hugh O'Byrne, an Irish Chieftain whose home was in the impregnable valley of Glenmalure.

Fiach, immediately sent a party to search for the two youths bringing with them food, drink and clothes. It was difficult to find them at first as it had snowed a lot during the night and one cliff face looked like another but finally they were located, covered with frozen hailstones. The two bodies huddled together under the frozen mass seemed more dead than alive, indeed Art, although alive then, died shortly after and was buried there. Aodh made a remarkable recovery but suffered severe frost bite of both feet. He later had both big toes amputated and was lame for the rest of his life.

As soon as Aodh had recovered fully he headed north. Travelling on horseback along with a small escort he crossed the Liffey right under the walls of Dublin Castle, for they knew well that every other crossing was closely guarded.
Among his escort were Phelim O'Toole and his brother. This was probably a gesture of reconciliation. Having accompanied him well north of Dublin, and so beyond the most dangerous part of his journey, the O'Tooles took their leave and returned south. Aodh was now in the care of Turlough Buí O'Hagan, one of the O'Neill's most trusted men. Turlough was also an excellent choice as he spoke the language of the English and was well acquainted with O'Neill's friends both Irish and English. Boldly travelling the main roads of Meath on two fine horses they reached the Boyne before morning. Here, rather than chance riding through Drogheda where they might le recognised they paid a fisherman to ferry them across in a currach and bring their horses via the town later in the day.
About two miles north of the river they visited and were entertained by Sir Garret Moore, an English Lord who was friendly with O'Neill. Having spent two days enjoying the hospitality of this gentleman, they continued their journey. They left after nightfall, and travelling all night and all next day, they made their next stop at the home of Turlough O'Neill of the Fews where they received a great welcome. They now felt safer as they were in O'Neill territory. Next day they reached Armagh and on the following day arrived in Dungannon where their host was Hugh O'Neill himself. Here Aodh was entertained secretly as O'Neill was still submissive to Dublin Castle. Four days and four nights he spent there and on leaving, was provided with an escort to protect him from robbers and woodkern, until he reached Lough Erne.

Here he was received by Maguire, Chief of Fermanagh who gave him the best of hospitality. Having rested here he travelled down the Lough by boat and on reaching the lower shore, where Belleek stands today, was met by a band of his own faithful and loyal people for he was now in his own country. They travelled to Ballyshannon, where the O'Donnells had a well-fortified castle. Here he was made welcome by many of his clansmen who had travelled from many parts of Tír Chonaill to meet him.

But all was not well in the land of Conall. For the past few years the English had gradually made many encroachments upon it, even taking up residence in O'Boyle's castle two miles from Donegal Town and closer still, in the Monastery (Abbey) only a few hundred yards from Donegal Castle. Thus Aodh found his native territory practically overrun by the enemy.

Immediately he commenced to assemble an army but before an engagement could take place the English departed after which the Brethern returned to the Monastery.

Aodh now had time to have his feet seen to and it was at this stage that the physicians decided to remove his toes as they couldn't cure them otherwise. By April when his wounds were almost healed he set about uniting his people. He assembled all those who were loyal to him at Kilmacrennan, O'Boyles, McSweeney Banagh, McSweeney Doe, McSweeney Fanat and many other smaller septs. Having held council, the nobles including 'O'Donnell' himself (since he was aware of his feebleness and advanced age) agreed to transfer the chieftaincy to Aodh Rua. On the third of May at the Rock of Doon as was customary Aodh was inaugurated and acclaimed, 'Ó Domhnaill.'

{Source: 'Beatha Aodha Ruaidh Uí Dhomhnaill' by Lughaidh O'Cléirigh]

Birmingham Tower, Dublin Castle

O'DONNELL OFFICERS

Under the Clan System, lesser Clans were delegated an office by a superior Clan. Here is a list of the smaller Clans and the offices they held from the O'Donnells.

MacRoartys, custodians of the 'Cathach'.
MacSweeneys, standard bearers and commanders of galloglasses.
O'Breslins, brehons (judges).
O'Clerys, historians and genealogist.
O'Dunlevys, physicians.
O'Friels, Chief inaugurators.
O'Gallaghers, commanders of cavalry.
Wards, poets.
O'Kerrigans, harpists.
O'Timoneys, cattle drovers.

Fuadach Aodh Rua

"Ó triallaigh liom ar bhord na loinge,"
Arsa an captain béalbhinn bréagach,
"Tá an téad go teann, faoi bhruach na mbeann,
Ar ucht Loch Súilí céimeach.

Tá an bhroinn líonlán d'fhíon na Spáinne,
Céad oigísead mór is tuilleadh,
Den digh is measúla i gcúirt an rí,
Beoir chroíúil chaoin gan mhilleadh.

Agus ólfaidh muid íocshláinte
As cornaibh óir araon,
Is beidh againn tamall cuideachta
Nach gcosnaíonn duitse pingin."

Thaitin comhrá an bhithiúnaigh
Go hansa le Aodh Rua,
Agus ar bhord na loinge, chuaigh sé amach,
Mo chreach is mo mhíle trua.

Ba tapaidh shiúl na bomaití
I measc imirtis is óil,
Ollghairdeas agus carthanas
Is mórán gléasraí ceoil.

Cuireadh agus freagraíodh ceisteanna
Os cionn na ngloiní lán,
Fan bhuaireamh ins an bhaile againn,
Agus gníomhairí thall sa Spáinn.

Agus na bristí fuilteacha a throidfí
Sula mbeadh duilliúr úr ar chrann,
Idir an bhanríon bhródúil Isibéal
Agus an Spáinneach uasal teann.

Agus nuair a ba mhian lenar gceannfort óg
A bheith ag dul chun an bhaile a luí,
Chuala a chluas an torman
A bhain léimneach as a chroí.

Bloic is rópaí callánach,
Ag cur seolta geala ar chrainn
Agus garbhghuth na mairnéalach
Ag déanamh gealgháire is grinn.

Is an long ina rith ar bharr na dtonn
Ag teitheadh roimh an tsíon,
Agus ba domhain amach san fharraige í
Nuair a nocht aníos an ghrian.

Ba tiubh a threabh sí a bealach
Thart timpeall Chondae an Dúin,
Agus arís gur leag sí a hancaire
Tráthnóna trasna an chuain.

Tá mac Iníon Duibh go huaigneach
Anocht i mBaile Átha Cliath,
A leaba lom ina leacacha'
Gan bhiotáilte no bhia.

Ach ainneoin é a bheith ceangailte
Le slabhraí fuar' go teann,
Tá ar namhaid nimhneach lagcroíoch
Le eagla roimh a lann.

Ainneoin ballaí arda agus bábhúin,
Slabhraí fuara agus glais lámh,
Agus airm tréan an ghárda
A fhaire oíche is lá.

Ach bhí cáirde i measc an namhad
Lán carthanais is croí,
A d'fhág Aodh is a chomrádaithe
Ina bhfir saora ins an tslí.

Bhí ábhar bróin i nDún na nGall
An oíche a fuadadh Aodh,
Ó Rath Maoláin síos an loch
Agus amach thar Ard Dún Rí.

Ach tá ábhar bróin inniu go fras
Ag Sassanaigh agus ag a gclann,
Nuair atá ar bprionsa óg sa bhaile again,
Ag cur faobhair ar a lann.

Is moch amárach a chluinfear,
Ó mhullach cnoc is glean,
Guth bródúil adharc Thír Chonaill
Ag cur cuireadh ar a clann.

Agus sin an cuireadh a fhreagrófar,
Ma freagraíodh aon chuireadh riamh,
Ó chladaigh chúil cois farraige,
Agus amach ar ucht na sliabh.

Anonn ó chnoic dhubha Inis Eoghain,
Agus ó ghaineamh bhán na dTuath,
Ó thír chnapánach na mBaoilleach
Go bruach an Easa Rua.

Tháinig said ina gcéadta,
Fir thréanmhar' riamh nar fheall,
Leis na sionnaigh agus na mic tire
A dhibírt amach as Dún na nGall.

Mar a scanraigh glam an iolair
An éanlaith ins na crainn,
Nó tafann toll na conairte
An giorria sa bhinn.

Nó búirtheach leoin na hainmhithe
As coillte coimhthíocha cúil,
Scanraigh Aodh na rógairí
Agus chuir go léir chun siúil.

Agus da nglacfaí a chomhairle an oíche sin
Roimh an bhriseadh bhrónach mhall,
Bheadh athrú dlí again
Ó Chionn tSáile go Dún na nGall.

The inscription on the headstone of the O'Donel plot in Kilconduff Cemetery (outside Swinford, Co. Mayo) reads as follows –

OLDCASTLE FAHYNESS 1701

◄─────────────────────────

O DONELS OF FAHYNESS

CHARLES son oc CALVAGH DUV & MARY O DONEL d. 1770 his son
HUGH O DONEL d. 1834 aged 84
his wife ELENA (nee JORDAN) of Roslevin d. 1822
MARY O BRIEN dau. of HUGH d. 1819
CECELIA O DONEL (nee JORDAN) Ballyhaunis
wife of EDMUND O DONEL son of HUGH d. 1835
ELEANOR O DONEL (nee BOURKE)
wife of IGNATIUS P> O DONEL son of HUGH d. 1839
CAPT. HUGH O DONEL son of IGNATIUS P. d. 1839
IGNATIUS P. O DONEL d. 1840
EDMUND O DONEL d. 1841
EDWARD O DONEL son of IGNATIUS P. d. 13th Mar 1849
MARY O DONEL (nee O BRIEN)
wife of EDWARD d. May 26th 1849
ELEANOR O DONEL wife of WILLIAM
son of IGNATIUS P. d. 1865
WILLIAM O DONEL d. 1867
EDWARD HUGH O DONEL son of EDWARD d. 1869
IGNATIUS P. O DONEL son of EDWARD d. 28th Aug. 1909
MARY O DONEL (nee COUGHLAN)
wife of IGNATIUS P. d. 15th Sept. 1921
MARIE O DONEL dau. of WILLIAM d. 12th May 1938
REV. EDWARD HUGH O DONEL son of IGNATIUS P. & MARY O DONEL
died 17th July 1914 SISTER MARY GERALD (Evelean) O DONEL
dr. of IGNATIUS P. & MARY O DONEL died 2nd March 1932
JOSEPHINE O DONEL dr. of IGNATIUS P. & MARY O DONEL died
16th Nov. 1957 GERALDINE O DONEL dr. of IGNATIUS P.
& MARY O DONEL died 1st Feb. 1958

LILE and PEADAR O DONNELL

These arms appear between the first two lines as indicated by the arrow.

Pilleadh Aodha Ruaidh Uí Dhomhnaill
(1592 A.D.)

Is líonta anocht atá 'Caisleán an Uisce,'
Is lonnrach gach fuinneog ó thalamh go díon;
Gidh farsaing an fíon ann, níl callán nó meisce
A' múscailt macalla na sean taobháin críon;
Tá sláintí da n-ól an ag taoisigh tréana
Do cheannphort a ndúiche tá leófa arís;
Ach ar maidin amárach le h-éirí na gréine,
Beidh slua níos mó ar an léana úd thíos.

Féach, cheanna tá 'n nuaidheacht thar mhór-leath na tire,
Tá teachtairí luthmhara a bualadh na slí,
A' dúiseacht tréan-spioraid a n-anamnacha fíora,
'S a' gríosadh na crógachta tá fós in gach croí.
Féach, féach, tá na tinte ar mhullach gach sléibhe
A' freagairt na bhfuagradh fríd dhubhacht is ceo,
Gidh dearg a lasadh, béidh pící 'gus claimhte
Níos deirge go luath i gcogadh níos teo.

Glóir, glóir a Thír Chonaill, le tréimhse gan chabhair,
Gur buach gach clan cróga ó'n Fhinn go Ros Eoghain,
Ar aghaidh libh a laochra, ó Mhálainn go Samhair,
Bíodh lúcháir anocht ag díbirt an bhróin.
Nach gcluintear an gáir úd ag líonadh na spéire
Mar thoirneach a' réabadh fríd chiúnas na ngleann?
Nach gcluintear guth fáilteach na ndaoine ag éirí?
Hurrá! Tá Aodh Ruadh arís os ár gcionn!

Níos sia na bígí is gruaim in bhur gcroí,
Tá dóchas a' briseadh ar Éirinn go léir;
Inné bhí an tsean chúis faoi néalta na hoíche
Amárach béidh dath úr ar fad ins an spéar.
Amárach béidh solas geal gréine ag sileadh
Ar chath-bhrat Thír Chonaill a' crathadh sa ghaoth,
Béidh na mílte fear tréan againn réidh le na mbuille,
Faoi arm is faoi éidiú da dtreorú ag Aodh.

Is díomhain le blianta bhí gliocas gach láimhe,
Is meirgeach a d'éirigh gach píc ar an chrann;
Ach bheathaigh an scríste smior úr in ár gcnámha,
'S d'fhág meirg an díomhaoinis níos géire gach lann.
Mar mhéaduigheas neart agus luathas na h-aibhne
Le fearthainn an Fhómhair indiaidh triomachta míos
Is amhlaidh bhéas sathadh ár sleagha níos doimhne
Nuair a chasfar na Sasanaigh orainn arís.

Ó! Taraidh go tapaidh, laoch coise 'gus marcach,
Ó chnocaibh is ghleannta ar fud Dhún na nGall,
Tá trom-chíos le h-íoc ag an tsean-namhad bheartach,
Ar fuath leis ar gcreideamh, is a rinne orainn feall.

Is fada gach fear dinn go foideach ag fanacht
Le pilleadh ár ngrá ghil ó Chaisleán Ath Cliath,
Chun buille a bhualadh, 's chun saoirse a cheannacht
Le daor-fhuil ar gcroí, ma 's toil é le Dia.

Na fanaidh! Tá cnámha shean-sinnsear Uí Dhomhnaill
Ag glaoch 'un díoltais ó lámha a gclann;
Beidh fiacha le h-íoc ag gach fear i dTír Chonaill
A fhad is tá lorg aon scriosadóir ann.
Le chéile! Le chéile! Béidh feallracht Loch Súiligh
Glan-nighte gan mhoill i bhfuil Sasanach teann;
Ar aghaidh! Ar aghaidh chun saoirse a mhílithe,
Tá 'n ceart ar ár dtaobh, is Aodh Ruadh ós ár gcionn.

Pádraig Ó Beirn as Málainn Beag a chum an dán seo. Cumadh é sna blianta roimh Éirí Amach na Cásca 1916 nuair a bhí Éirinn faoi dhaor-smacht Gall agus is chun spiorad agus misneach a spreagadh in óige na tire a cumadh é agus píosaí eile da leithiéid.

Red Hugh O'Donnell's Address
to his Soldiers before the Battle of the Curlew Mountains.

Brother chiefs, and clansmen loyal, tried in many a bloody fray;
God be thanked these robber Saxons come to meet us here to-day.
Boasting Clifford, Essex minion, swears he'll make the rebels flee-
We will give him hearty greeting, like to that at Ashanee. (1)
What, though traitor Celts oppose us - be their number three to one?
Greater glory to Clan Connell, when this tough day's work is done.
Shrived at Holy Mass this morning, danger we may fearless dare;
For we draw the sword of justice, shielded all in faith and prayer.
Not for conquest, or for vengeance, on this blessed Lady Day,
Not in strength or numbers trusting, do we face their proud array;
But for Holy Mary's honour, by their tainted lips defiled,
For the sacred rights of freemen, for the mother, maid, and child.
Prone and bleeding lies our country, sorrow clouds her crownless brow,
All the lines of peerless beauty limned in ghastly colours now.
In the light of glories olden beaming through our dark disgrace,
See the maddening wrongs and insults heaped upon our fallen race!
Roofless homestead, broken altar, slaughtered priest, discoloured maid –
Children of an outraged mother, whet ye well the thirsty blade.
Scorning rock and brushwood cover, rush like swooping eagles forth,
Hard and home push every pike-head, sinewy steersmen of the North!
Cleave in twain the lustful Saxon, tame Dunkellin's soaring pride,
Smite the double-souled O'Connors - traitors false to every side. (2)
Down upon them, Banagh's chieftain, sweep their ranks your spears before,
As the North wind sweeps the stubble through the gap of Barnes-More.
Forward! Forward! Brave McDermott, strike for fair Moylurg's domain,
For yon lake in beauty sleeping, for the holy island's fane. (3)
Strike! and drive the swinish Saxon, herding in their sacred shade,
Far from Boyle's old abbey cloisters, where your father's bones are laid.
Holy Virgin! we implore thee, by that abbey's rifled shrine, (4)
Columcille of Doire Calgach, patron of O'Donnell's line, (5)
Good St. Francis! for the glory of thy name in Donegal,
Speed ye now Tirconnell's onset, till we rout them one and all.
Should O'Donnell fall in combat - if the foe be forced to yield,
Better death I never pray for, than to fall upon the field,
Where the cause of Erin triumphed, and the Saxon was laid low,
With that green flag floating o'er me, and my face against the foe.
Never chieftain of Clan Dalaigh to th'invader bowed the knee;
By the black years of my bondage, it shall never be done to me.
I would rather angry ocean rolled o'er castle, cot, and hall,
Than see any Saxon bodach rule in royal Donegal.
Deathless fame in song and story will enshroud the men who died,

Fighting God's and freedom's battle bravely by O'Donnell's side.
Great will be his need of glory, honoured long the victor's name,
Pointing proudly to her kinsman, many a maid will tell his fame;
'Lo! he fought at Doonaveragh,' aged men will whispering say,
And make way before the altar for the heroes of to-day.
Gleaming bright through darkening ages will this great day's memory glide.
Like the Saimer's bright-wav'd waters glancing onward to the tide.

This battle was fought on the 15th August, 1599, the Irish were commanded by Red Hugh and other chieftains; the English by Sir Conyers Clifford, Governor of Connaught. Before the battle, according to the Four Masters, O'Donnell, who had the day before fasted in honour of the Blessed Virgin, 'as he was wont to do …….caused Mass to be celebrated for himself and the forces in general, and after making his confession and rigidly repenting of his sins, he received the Eucharist, and commanded his forces to pray to God fervently for the salvation of their souls in the first place, and to deliver them from the great danger which awaited them from the English,' He then addressed a stirring harangue to his soldiers in the Irish language (given at length in O'Sullivan Beare's, 'Ireland under Elizabeth'), the substance which is expressed in the above verses. O'Donnell was completely victorious; Sir Conyers Clifford, many of his officers, and nearly 1500 of his men were killed on the field or in the flight. The Four Masters add, 'That the army offered up thanks to God and the Blessed Virgin Mary for the victory, and the unanimous voice of the men was, that it was not by the force of arms the English were defeated, but by the supplication of O'Donnell and his forces, after he had received the Body and Blood of Christ in the beginning of that day after his fast the previous day in honour of the Blessed virgin.'

1 . Ashanee - Ballyshannon, where O'Donnell routed Clifford and his forces on Lady Day, two years earlier.
2. O'Connor Don and O'Connor Roe on this occasion, not for the first time, joined the English.
3. Lough Cé, at the foot of the Curlews, in which was a monastery dedicated to the Holy Trinity.
4. The Cistercian Abbey of Boyle was dedicated to the Blessed Virgin.
5. Doire Calgach - the oak grove of Calgach - the ancient name of Derry.

Red Hugh's March to Kinsale

A synoptic version of a lecture given by Capt. Joe O'Kane to the county Donegal Historical Society in the Abbey Hotel, Donegal Town on 9th March, 1984.

Hugh O'Donnell was at Ballymote Castle (then in his possession) when the decision was made to go to the assistance of the beleaguered Spaniards in Kinsale. A proclamation was issued to his forces to assemble at Ballymote and hasty preparations here made. The way to Kinsale was long, wet and marshy with little or no roadways and heavy opposition could be expected.

They travelled light, each man carrying his own weapon and food rations (oaten bread, butter, salt etc.). Few horses, cumbersome carriages or canons were brought.

Having celebrated the Feast of Samhain (Halloween), Hugh O'Donnell reviewed his troops clan by clan and on the 2nd November, 1601 began the march south.

On leaving Ballymote, they travelled in a south-easterly direction along a road still known as 'Bothar an Iarla Ruaidh' that leads in the direction of the Curlew Hills. They passed close to Lough Key avoiding Boyle (as it may have been garrisoned) and on to Elphin, a total of 30 miles, the first day.

Next day they marched south through Roscommon and crossed the Suck without difficulty. Avoiding Athlone and Shannon Bridge, they forded the Shannon at Shannon Harbour - Athlone was fortified. Having crossed the Shannon, they met their first hostilities. It came from MacCoughlan, through whose lands they were travelling. This action proved costly for MacCoughlan as the Northmen ravished, plundered, burned and destroyed most of his property.

Travelling south-east through Kinnity, they crossed over Slieve Bloom (mountains) and down through the village of Bellaghmore, reaching Drumsaileach near Templemore where they camped on the 6th or 7th of November. Here they awaited the arrival of O'Neill's forces. For three weeks they waited, during which time they ravaged and plundered the countryside around them in search of food, as armies did in those days.

The English had expected that O'Neill and O'Donnell would come to the aid of the Spaniards - on the 17th November they were sure of it when they learned of O'Donnell's position near Templemore. Next day they debated in council what action to take. Eventually, Sir George Carew with 4, 000 horse and foot was sent to intercept O'Donnell. By the 21st November, Carew reached Ardmoyle (north of Cashel and south of Holy Cross) and camped there. Both armies continued to spy on each other but made no attempt at an engagement. The distance separating them was four miles. On the 30th November, O'Donnell visited Holy Cross Abbey where he venerated a relic of the true cross and headed back to camp next day.

O'Donnell, by now, knew he would soon have to move as food was becoming scarce and his position becoming more precarious each day. Carew was joined by another regiment under

Sir Christopher St. Laurence. Carew believed he had the only road south blocked so he was prepared to sit and wait. O'Donnell wouldn't be as foolhardy as to make an encircular movement by going east because of the proximity of the English forces heading south.

On the night that Hugh O'Donnell visited Holy Cross the river Suir was in high spate (the whole of that November was extremely wet) but the next night hard frost set in, the likes of which had rarely been seen in Ireland before. O'Donnell took advantage of the weather conditions and set out over the Slieve Felim Mountains. Slieve Felim was considered impossible in winter but with the unusual frost and the help of trusty guides it became just possible.

Before leaving camp, O'Donnell employed the age-old trick of having local people keep the fires burning all night and create the usual hustle and bustle of an occupied camp.

This ploy deceived Carew's spies and so precious time was gained for O'Donnell's troops, who travelling light as already mentioned, traversed slippery but hard mountain paths, covering a total of 22 Irish mites (1 Irish mile = 2240 yards) of rough mountain terrain in one night. By early morning they were on the south side of Slieve Felim, close to Abbington, but still they did not rest. They marched all next day, covering another 12 Irish miles. That night they camped close to Croom.

When Carew learned that O' Donnell had departed he decided to quit camp and try to cut him off on the south side of Slieve Felim, but when Carew reached Abbington at 11 o'clock he was amazed to find that his adversary had already marched through - he was further amazed when he learned that they hadn't stopped till they reached Croom.

Carew declared that there was no way he could hope to catch up with such a fleet-footed enemy and later remarked that it was the greatest march ever recorded or even heard of. So he gave up the chase and returned to Kinsale arriving there on 6th December.

O'Donnell rested briefly at Croom where he spent the night in the Countess of Kildare's castle. He then crossed the Maigue (river) into the Barony of Connelagh where he camped

for a week. Again he plundered the countryside in search of food.
Now the Fitzmaurices in this area of Kerry had lost all their castles to Carew. So when O'Donnell arrived, he and Fitzmaurice took the opportunity of attacking the Carew-held fortresses and succeeded in regaining many of them.

The march was resumed on the 10th December passing through and around Slieve Luchra, through Muskerry and Dunhollow and on down the valley of the Bandon to Innishannon which they reached about the 15th December, 1601. Here the arrival of O'Neill's forces was awaited and the joint armies camped there for one day; their combined strength is said to have numbered 5,500 along with 500 Munstermen. They now moved to Belgooley and camped in a large field on the 16th December. This field is three miles north east of Kinsale.

Here they remained until 31st December when at nightfall they moved to the hill of Coolcarron, bringing them in sight of the English camp. Early on the morning of the 3rd January 1602 they made their final and fateful move when they advanced into battle - a battle which ended in disaster for them and was to be the death of Gaelic Ireland.

Other Ulster and Connaught Clans that marched to Kinsale.
O'Rourke, MacSweeney of Doe, O'Doherty, O'Cahan, O'Boyle, Mac Donagh, MacDermot, O'Kelly, O'Beirne, O'Connor, Burke, O'Hara, Maguire.
Munster Clans: Fitzmaurice, Fitzthomas, MacCarthy.

Red Hugh's Seal as it appears on letters to King Philip

The Last Will of Red Hugh O'Donnell.

When, almost a century ago, Fr. Denis Murphy, S.J., was preparing his edition of O Cleirigh's 'Life of Aodh Rua', he discovered a copy of part of Red Hugh's will in the archives of Simancas. We are indebted to Fr. John J. Silke for locating the entire will in the Archive of Valladolid University. This document was drawn up, shortly before Red Hugh's death, by the notary Domingo de Albiz, Fr. Florence Conry, O.F.M. (1560 - 1629) acting as translator and interpreter.

Here is an English translation prepared by Fr. Silke and first published by him in Studia Hibernica, no. 24 (1984-8)

Testamento del Conde Adonel yrlandes   Septiembre 1602

Yn Dei nomine, amen. Sepan quantos esta carta de testamento ultima y por est a mera voluntad vieren, como yo el Conde Adonell de Yrlanda ....

In the name of God, Amen. Let these who shall see this last will and testament know that I, Lord O 'Donnell of Ireland, being in bed, infirm in body of that illness which the Lord God has visited upon me, but sound in mind, with what judgment He was pleased to endow me, fearful of death, as is natural to my creaturely condition, and believing as a faithful and Catholic Christian in all that the holy mother Church of Rome holds and believes, do testify - and I know that I make and ordain this my testament to the praise and honour of God our Lord and of the glorious Virgin Mary His mother, whom I take and hold for my lady and advocate in all my acts and whom I beg and supplicate to pray for my soul, which I commend to her - and I make my said testament in the following manner:

Firstly, I offer my soul to my God and Lord Jesus Christ, Who bought and redeemed it with His precious and blessed blood, that He too be pleased to pardon me and raise me to His holy glory at His good pleasure, Amen.

Next, I commend my body 'to the clay of which it was formed, and I wish and order that it be interred in the church of the monastery of the Lord Saint Francis in Valladolid (erased: 'particular spot which the King our Lord shall appoint. And may his will be done in everything').

Item, I now on the point of death, without hope of returning to the world, say and declare that I take God for witness that I do not say anything here contrary to the truth. I appoint and name my brother Don Rury O'Donnell as my heir to all my estates, lands, lordships, and vassals, whichsoever may be, to inherit, hold and enjoy them, now and in perpetuity, in manner and form according to law: such is my will.

Item, I entrust the said Don Rury my brother and Don Cathbharr my youngest brother jointly, with all my inheritance, to His Majesty's protection and grace.

Item, I declare that I take God for witness that the king our lord did not, and as I think will not, have in Ireland so loyal and faithful a servant as I, or one who would so often adventure his person in His Majesty's service. Next, I declare that the province of Connacht, which lies within my borders, was at the beginning of this war subject to the queen. I then laid it waste and conquered it, without help from anyone in the said province, except for some persons expelled from their territories in the said province, whom I took into my pay. It is unnecessary to detail here the other services which I rendered His Majesty in every part of Ireland.

Item, I declare that, as His Majesty knows, peace treaties were agreed between the Irish and the queen of England. But I undid them all, in order to serve God and His Majesty and to make me and my heirs his vassals.

Item, I declare that in case Lord O'Neill – as I think and consider he will not do – should wish to violate the treaties and agreements determined and made between Lord O'Neill and me and my heirs, I charge His Majesty to maintain my brother in the king's service and in my brother's rights.

Item, I say and declare that among the heads of treaties there is one which is that all the help, aid, or grace that His Majesty may give or send to Lord O'Neill and me, should be divided in two equal parts, and that the same should hold among our heirs. The stipulation was that one had no pre-eminence over the other and that in walking or travelling together whichever was the elder should be on the right hand. I humbly beseech His Majesty to support my brother in conformity with the said treaty and (so as to keep him the more beholden) to give him some commission and if it seems good to His Majesty to pay him some salary.

Item, I declare and say that Don Redmond de Burgo, baron of Leitrim, who came here in my company, is a gentleman of note and has performed eminent services. Knowing his bravery and his ability to render important services to the king, I commend him to His Majesty, who may take it that he is very worthy of his patronage and is utterly reliable. Also I commend my confessor, Father Florence Conry, to the king, begging him to provide him with some Irish bishopric, even should the Father be unwilling to undertake this burden. This will redound to the service of God and of His Majesty and will be for the common good of Ireland, since he is so holy a man and so very greatly experienced in Irish affairs. I humbly charge His Majesty to give order to consult him on Irish matters. And I say that His Majesty will be very well served to send the said Father as soon as possible to Ireland. He is highly regarded by all those lords [i.e. of the Confederacy], who value his counsel very much and who will pluck up courage at his arrival there.

I also recommend Matthew Tully, my secretary, to His Majesty's bounty. He has been a very loyal servant to me, hard-working and diligent. Knowing that my prayers must carry great weight with His Majesty, I am confident that his case for recompense will be considered. However handsome the award, he has earned it in full. I vouch for the loyalty of his service to His Majesty, his correct behaviour, and his knowledge of and expert skill in Irish affairs. I therefore beg His Majesty to provide that he be consulted in Irish business, and I assure His Majesty that he will not be deceived. Meanwhile I beg His Majesty to send money and some troops to Ireland to Lord O'Neill and to my brother before the notice of my death arrives. Otherwise they will be lost, for as soon as that news arrives there they will all hasten to make peace with the English. For they had pinned all their hopes on the aid I was to bring them, and they would be reanimated if letters from the king, together with the money, were to anticipate word of my death. I also declare that there is with me a boy called Don Gelasio, my nephew; and I beg His Majesty to support him and – until they find embarkation to take them to my brother – my gentlemen and servants at Corunna. I also make bold to charge His Majesty to pay what little debt I owe in Spain: a hundred ducats to General Pedro de Zubiaur, another hundred to an Irish merchant named Nicholas Lynch, who is in the city of Corunna, and eighty ducats to Edward Eustace, an Irish gentleman also in Corunna.

Again I beg and implore His Majesty for alms (seeing I have not a real), so that some masses may be said for my soul. And I beg His Majesty that, after God our Lord has taken me from this world to the next, he give order to bury me in the said monastery of the Lord Saint Francis in the city of Valladolid with interment in keeping with the quality of my person, and with the masses ordered by His Majesty. I beg him, as so Christian and good a king and lord, to do so; and in his royal hands I leave whatever has to be done in this. And I revoke and cancel and give for nothing whatever will or wills I have before this made in writing or orally, and I desire that they be not valid or have faith in legal decision or out of it, except this which at present I do and ordain. I wish that it be carried out and be valid in legal decision and outside of it, and if it is not valid for my testament that it be valid for my codicil, and if it is not valid for my codicil that it be valid for my last will and by this mere will or in that way and form which may have legal standing. In testimony of which I make this said testament before Diego de Albiz, notary of the king, and the witnesses subscribing below, in the town of Simancas, on the seventh day of the month of September, in the year one thousand six hundred and two, there being present as witnesses Doctor John Ninan, Irishman, physician, and Matthew Tully and Maurice Ultach and Father Maurice Ultach and Francisco de Aguilar, all Irishmen, who know the language of Ireland and who declare themselves to be natives of Ireland, being present in the said town, and who swore in legal form in the hands of me, the present notary, in accordance with law, that they know Lord O'Donnell and that he is the same who is present and is of the same name written here. And the same lord signed his name in this register. And since I, the said notary, neither know nor understand the Irish language, which is that which the said testator speaks, for the making of this said testament Father Florence Conry translated the said language into Castilian. Father Conry explained to the said testator everything contained in the said testament and also wrote and composed the translation. And the said witnesses who also know the said language, obliged by the same oath, declared that the said interpreter translated and repeated all that the said testator uttered, which is the same which is contained in this said testament.

As witnesses also there were Juan de Albiz, Bachelor, and Juan Fernandez de Camara, servants of His Majesty, and Pedro de Monsalvo, present in the said town, who saw the said testator sign; and also the said interpreter signed; and the said testator, although he began to sign, did not, because of the gravity of his illness, sign, because he could not. (stet: the particular spot which the king our lord shall appoint. And may his will be done in everything.)

(Signatures:) Aodh O I, F. Florencio Conrio

Tax: 4 reals
Before me,

Domingo de Albiz (Rubrica)

Death of Aodh Rua

by V. O'Donnell

After the defeat of Kinsale, Aodh Rua, the famous Red Hugh O'Donnell, went to Spain to solicit help from King Philip. However, neither Aodh nor Spanish aid was destined to come to Ireland. Aodh died on the 10th September, 1602 at Simancas, aged 30 years.

With the news of his death came the rumour that he was poisoned by one James Blake from Galway, acting as an English agent. This theory was accepted by both English and Irish until the present century – The English because they liked to believe that a traitor was safe nowhere; the Irish because it was a further indication of English treachery.

In 1945 a team of Irish research workers was sent to Simancas, Spain to report on documents of Irish interest there. To expect to find documentary evidence of Aodh Rua's death among 33 million documents in the short time allotted, was like expecting to find the proverbial needle in a haystack – yet, they did.

Several documents were found making reference to his death, all written by people either present during his illness and death, or by people who got their information from those who were.

The following belong to the first category:

Dr. Juan Nynan (Sean O Naoidheanain), an Irish Doctor working in Spain at the time who was present during the whole of O'Donnell's illness, along with Dr. Alveraz, the King's own doctor. Matthew Tully (Matha O Maolthuile), O'Donnell's secretary at home and in Spain who was with him until the very end, as was Fr. (afterwards Archbishop) Florence Conry O. F. M., O'Donnell's confessor.

Belonging to the second category is:- Hugh O'Neill, who wrote several letters from Rome to King Philip of Spain pleading the Irish cause and recounting the injustices at the hands of the English.

In all of these documents there is not one mention of poisoning but rather death from natural causes. All their accounts agree that his illness lasted 17 days (baoi fri re secht la ndecc ina licche) and that a few days before his death he vomited a huge worm, from which evidence we conclude that he died from tapeworm, a disease quite prevalent in those days. To the Irish of the time, even had they known this, it is quite understandable that such a common death for a great hero was unbecoming, hence the acceptance of the poisoning theory.

The Vatican archives contain documents of further corroborative evidence such as letters from Fr. Lugi Mansoni S.J., Nuncio to Ireland who was delayed at Valladolid at the time of Aodh's illness and death. From these letters we get an account similar to those already mentioned.

Fr. Donagh Mooney O.F.M., who was personally acquainted with Aodh Rua, has left us a vivid pen-picture of him. Fr. Mooney would have met Fr. Conry, Matthew Tully and another eye-witness, Fr. Maurice Dunleavy, shortly afterwards, but Mooney makes clear his belief that O'Donnell's death was due to natural causes.

Lughaidh O Cleirigh was what might be called Aodh's official biographer yet he states merely that his fatal illness seized him at Simancas where he died on 10th September, 1602 after 17 days illness.

The Four Masters, admirers of the O'Donnels as they were, would also presumably have been glad to mention how Aodh Rua met his death by English treachery if in the intervening years that fact had been known, but instead they have nothing to add

Simancas Castle, Spain

to the account given by Lughaidh O Cleirigh which they merely transcribed. Indeed Fr. Maurice Dunleavy, who stood by the bedside of the dying chieftain and was one of the signatories to the preface to the Annals, lived with the Four Masters by the River Drowes while they compiled the Annals and must have often spoken of the death of one of the greatest O'Donnell chieftains 'in a high castle room in courtly Spain.'

But what of James Blake? The truth is that he did set out on a mission to eliminate Aodh Rua but it was not unknown to Aodh and those around him. Blake would have had little chance in getting near him much less to administer the fatal poison. But as soon as the news of Aodh's death arrived in England it was assumed that it was Blake's work and it was from here the rumour originated. No official English document confirms the poisoning theory nor is there any record of Blake receiving a reward for his services.

To sum up about the death of Aodh Rua:
1. There is no reliable evidence that he was poisoned by an English agent.
2. His death was probably due to natural causes.
3. There is evidence that high English officials and even Queen Elizabeth herself were not above approving a plot to kill him by treachery.

4. There is sufficient evidence that James Blake of Galway set out from Ireland for Spain with the intention and encouragement of Sir George Carew to kill Aodh Rua.
Some quotations about his death:
'..... O'Donnell himself, partly through sorrow, partly through the intemperateness of air and climate, to which he was not accustomed, fell ill and succumbed in a short time, dying in the month of September.'
Fr. Donagh Mooney, O.F.M. - 1617.
'In Spain in the meantime an army was being prepared which would have been sent over to Ireland with O'Donnell only that most unfortunately he died. When the news of his death became known, it filled Rory's companions with grief and despair of any help from Spain.'
Philip O'Sullivan - 1621
'On his way thither he was taken ill at Simancas, and, sixteen days later, on 10th September, he died. He was buried with the highest honours in the chapter of the Monastery of St.

Francis at Vallodolid. Carew, who knew that an Irishman had gone to Spain with the intention of killing him, thought that he had been poisoned, but this is highly unlikely.'
Prof. Cyril Falls (recent publication)

'Heartbroken by this, he took to bed of a fever which suddenly grew serious but then improved somewhat; . . . . . . he grew gradually worse and finally passed away.'
Fr. Luigi Mansoni S.J. - 1602

'There goeth withall a report here that a kind of snake or serpent was found within him. It may be that he was troubled with the worm, as many children and men be . . . . .'
Doctor's Report-1602

'On his deathbed he begged St. Francis' habit, in which he was buried, and he begged it with the intention of renouncing the world, had it pleased God to restore him to health.'
Fr. Donagh Mooney, O.F.M. -1617

[Source: Rupert S. O Cochlain notes. See also Donegal Annual 1994, 'Aodh Rua Ó Domhnaill – What caused his death?' by Conall Mac Cuinnragáin.]

Róisín Dubh

A Róisín, ná bíodh brón ort fár éiri duit.
Tá na bráithre ag teacht thar sáile is iad ag triall ar muir.
Tiocfaidh do phárdún ón bPápa is ón Róimh anoir
Is ní spárálfar fíon Spáinneach ar mo Róisín dubh.

Is fada an réim do lig mé léi ó inné go dtí inniu.
Trasna sléibhte go ndeachas léi fé sheolta ar muir
Is an Éirne do caith mé de léim í cé mór an sruth
Is bhí ceol téad ar gach taobh díom is mo Róisín dubh.

Beidh an Éirne ina tuillte tréana is réabfar cnoic,
Beidh an fharraige ina tonnta dearga is doirtear fuil,
Beidh gach gleann sléibhe ar fud Éireann is móinte ar crith
Lá éigin sula n-éaga mo Róisín dubh.

Focla dóchais ó Aodh Rua chuig Éire is é ar leabaigh an bhais, curtha i bhfiliocht ag Eoghan Rua Mac an Bhaird.

Façade of Franciscan Monastery, Valladolid where Aodh Rua was buried.

Aodh Mac Aodh Dubh of Ramelton

By Séamus Mac Aoidh, Falcarrach

Aodh Mac Aodh Dubh, or Aodh Óg Dubh(3), as he is sometimes called, was the greatest of the Ramelton O'Donnels. A brother of Manus the 21st Chieftain, he is described as 'Glún deirneach gaiscidh Gael' or 'The Achilles of the Irish Race.' He was very partial to fast horses. His own horse and those of his cavalry, according to tradition, had to be: '. . .big, sound, young, noble, high-headed, load-carrying, lively-hearted, broad-breasted, haughty, easy-bearing, sleek. . .' Then to discover if the horse was '. . . perfectly sound, easy-ridden, obedient . . .' the animal, bearing the rider, was made to swim across the Lennon about opposite the castle (where the river is widest). The horse that dashed most daringly into the stream and swan across the quickest was chosen.

Aodh was junior, almost certainly, to his stepbrother, Manus(2), who was inaugurated Chieftain in 1537. It is highly unlikely that Aodh became Tanist then as historians estimate that he was an only child of one year of age at the time. When eventually he became Tanist and was in direct line for the title of Chief he was unfortunately forestalled by An Calbhach (4) who had Manus, his father, imprisoned and himself elevated to the position of Chief. When An Calbhach died suddenly in 1566 Aodh must surely have thought his opportunity had come to be declared 'An Dalach.' But to his disappointment, Aodh Dubh (5) or Aodh Mac Manus succeeded as Taoiseach. Aodh was disappointed once more when Aodh Dubh resigned in favour of his son Red Hugh (12). When Red Hugh died in Spain nobody had the political clout to nominate the Ramelton hero. In the following year Niall Garbh (16) took advantage of the political vacuum and disarray that followed Kinsale and had himself unofficially inaugurated.

Three times the opportunity arose; three times was Aodh snubbed. Even the English by-passed his just claim when they created Rory (13) Earl of Tirconnell. When Red Hugh was inaugurated Aodh refused to attend the ceremony at the Rock of Doon, but later mollified and offered his fealty to the young Chieftain. It was important to Red Hugh to have the Ramelton man on his side for it was said of him: 'This Aodh mac Aodha Duibh was a distinguished noble. He was a handsome good-looking man, a well brought up knowledgeable person of fine physique; he was experienced in the best manners of that time, pleasant in peace and brave in battle. He was a generous host, amiable with his neighbours, ferocious in fight, harsh with the enemy yet humane with them in victory. His name was on everyone's lips throughout Ireland and his characteristics were compared with those of the great. It was said of him that he had the acumen of Lubhaidh Lamhfhada, was as skilled in the weapons of war as Cuchulainn, as deadly in battle as Conall Cearnach, as good a horse-rider as Troilus, son of Priam. During his lifetime he had never suffered defeat either in battle or single combatant.'

When Red Hugh began his campaign against the English he had the full support of the Ramelton man. Aodh of Ramelton had proven his worth in battle before when he assisted

Red Hugh's father at Farsetmore in 1567. However, in spite of Aodh's many attributes Seán Óg O'Doherty was the one Red Hugh chose as second-in-command followed by Niall Garbh (16). The Maguire was put in charge of cavalry. Did Red Hugh consider him too old at 60 or did he not trust him? Aodh Mac Aodh Dubh must have accompanied Red Hugh on his many raiding expeditions into Connacht. The story is told in the Ramelton neighbourhood that he was once captured by the enemy when he outrode his cavalry while pursuing the defeated and, in his haste, found himself trapped alone in Sligo Castle. Aodh's fame as a horseman had evidently proceeded him, for the Captain of the Guard, himself a horseman of note, challenged him to a 'duel' in horsemanship. Aodh would accept the challenge on one condition only, that his son be contacted and told to bring to the castle his 'lean swift steed.' His wish was complied with; one bright morning son and horse arrived. Aodh mounted and sped around the yard putting on such show of horsemanship as the company had never seen. Then while the English were still enjoying the dexterity and skill of horse and rider, Aodh pulled his son up behind him and made the horse clear the prison wall and sped to freedom. How much truth there is in that story I cannot say.

'With one great leap they cleared the wall,
The jail left far behind,
With mouth agape the sergeant stood –
The feat had stunned his mind;
Too late to chase the flying hooves,
Too late the bugle call,
For back once more to Lennon shore
Sped Hugh of Donegal.'

Once while accompanying Red Hugh in Connacht, Sir Henry Docwra ensconced himself and his men in Culmore from whence he made many damaging forays on the surrounding territory of Inishowen. When Red Hugh returned he chose a large body of soldiers and a troop of horse (Aodh of Ramelton was among the latter). The English grazed their horses outside the city of Derry and Red Hugh resolved to capture the horses thus rendering the English incapacitated. 'In the darkness of the night' Red Hugh prepared an ambush. Leaving the main body hiding in a gorge of a steep cliff on the mountain slope to the north of the city, he placed a few of his cavalry beside the city gates.

Early in the morning as the horses were being brought out to the fields O'Donnell's horsemen vigorously attacked the drovers and made off with the horses. Immediately the alarm was raised in the city Docwra and those of his men still with horses gave chase. As Red Hugh reached the gorge he ordered the horses to be taken to a secure place while he and the rest of his men gave battle to the pursuers. The fighting was furious. According to the Four Masters Hugh of Ramelton 'made a well-aimed cast of a javelin at the General, Sir Henry Docwra, and striking him directly in the forehead, wounded him very severely. When the General was thus pierced, he turned back, and the English, seeing their chief, their adviser, and their mighty man, wounded, returned home in sorrow and disgrace, and pursued their horses no further.'

Aodh's caslte at Ramelton was built by Neachtain O'Donnell, Chief of Tír Chonaill (1439-'52) for one of his sons, possibly Ruadhraí (1452 -'54). Docwra, in writing of this castle says: 'It is the meetest and most commodious of any other upon the neck of the country and for the defence thereof.'

The castle fell to Docwra in 1601. Aodh's attempt to regain it failed. However, under the Plantation of Ulster, he received his castle back along with a grant of 1,000 acres of his own land for life. The rest of his land went to the planters as did the rent thereof.

When he died around 1618 Aodh Mac Aodha Duibh was an octogenarian and had witnessed many hapless scenes that blotted the North-Western landscape. The abrupt and uneasy transition from the old order to the new and the chill foreign wind that blew along the corridors of the Gaelic world brought nothing but despondency and lost hope. When Aodh died, with him died the last remaining hope of the Gael.

LIEUTENANT-GENERAL CHARLES H. O'DONNELL

Charles O'Donnell was born on the 3rd. Sept. 1857 in Jujuy in the very north of Argentina. His father was Dr. Sabino O'Donnell, a Federal Government Minister of that province, his mother was Dona Josefa Perez. Sabino's grandfather (of the Spanish line) was sent from Spain in the middle of the eighteenth century to create the Academy of Mathematics in what was then called the Vice-royalty of the Rio de la Plata. Charles joined the army at a very early age and saw much action in the civil and frontier wars that raged in the country at the time. The country known as Argentina today was then taking shape but with much resistance. The Central Government of the time had much trouble quelling continuous local rebellions by the natives and it was here with the 12th Battalion, Border Infantry that young O'Donnell saw his first action. In Dec. 1870 he entered the newly created Military Academy in Buenos Aires. A year later he was back in service with the same 12th Batt. He was, once again, much involved in the campaign to unify Argentina which often meant subduing minor resistance by local tribes who resented and resisted any infringement of their territories by, what they considered, foreign rule.

O'Donnell's greatest contribution to this campaign was the part he played in opening up the Patagonia for colonization. This was a large triangle of land stretching from Buenos Aires right down to the very south of the continent. This territory was an uninviting land, with the second highest mountains in the world, much desert, and populated by Indian tribes who were inhospitable to the white man. The only white men there at the time were Welsh whalers living on the coast just opposite the Malvino Islands.

O'Donnell suppressed all resistance offered by the native tribes, and so brought, this vast area under Argentine rule, including that area held by the whalers whom he forced to obey Argentine laws and sing its National Anthem. News reached Britain somewhat altered. It was reported in London that a colony of British whalers in South America was attacked by marauding Irishmen led by an O'Donnell.

Needless to say promotion followed success and Charles received much of the latter. Indeed he was always on the winning side. By 1886 he was made Lieut-colonel and Chief of the 1st. Infantry Batt. Later that year he was raised to Colonel. In 1893 he was nominated director of the Military Academy and in 1896 Chief of the 2nd. Batt. of the Buenos Aires Division. In 1900 he was made a member of the Committee of the Council of War, an office he exercised only for a year, when more important posts came along. These included Inspector of Infantry, Director of the School for Potential Officers, and the Campo de Mayo in which capacity he rose to General of Brigade in 1904.

In May 1910 he was assigned Aide-de-Camp to the president of Chile during the centenary celebrations. In August of that year he was promoted to General and took command of the 5th Division, a post he filled with the distinction that characterised all the acts of his military career. He retired on the 30th April 1917 a 5-star General after 59 years and 19 days of military service. General Charles Henry O'Donnell died in Buenos Aires on the 22nd. Sept. 1927. He had been married to Felisa Rosa Suarez and had 15 children, 11 of which survived.

(The above is translated from 'Biografias ArgentinasY Sudamericanas' p. 190 – 194 with some remarks by Guillermo O'Donnel1.)

Hugh O'Donnell of Larkfield

by Rupert S. Ó Cochlain

The Plantation of Ulster and the Cromwellian Settlement marked the dispersal of the surviving O'Donnells of Tyrconnell. Rory of Lifford (22), grandson of Niall Garbh O'Donnell (16) who was committed to the Tower of London in 1609 for 'complicity in O'Doherty's rebellion' of the previous year, and who died in 1626, removed to Mayo with a large train of followers sometime prior to 1664. A kinsman of his, Connell O'Donnell (24) who was married to Rory's daughter was more tenacious and succeeded in retaining a foothold in the home territory after the exodus to Connaught. The family was still reasonably affluent. Connell is recorded as Titulado of the district of Ballkergan, Altepast, Aghevay, Letterbricke, Ballinbonibany and Ballibonitem, all in the civil parish of Stranorlane (Stranorlar) in the 1659 Census. His son, Hugh (27), married Flora Hamilton, daughter of John Hamilton of Killanure, Convoy, Co. Donegal, by whom he had three children. Following her death in 1716 he married Margaret, daughter of Hugh Montgomery, of Derrygonnelly, Co. Fermanagh, who presented him with a second family.

John O'Donovan tells us that Hugh left Donegal for Mullaghbane near the head of Lough Macnean, Co. Fermanagh, after the collapse of the Jacobite cause, and shortly afterwards settled at Larkfield, Manorhamilton, Co. Leitrim. The dates of the second marriage and the taking up of his residence at both Mullaghbane and Larkfield are unknown. It should be remembered that the O'Donnells were no longer freeholders. Non-renewal of leases could have precipitated his move to Fermanagh. The fact that his second wife was from there suggests that he was already living at Mullaghbane much longer than recorded by O'Donovan. All would appear to have been going well until a Protestant 'discoverer', one Rowland Kane of Desertmartin, Co. Derry availing of the penal enactment of 1709, filed a Bill of Discovery against him in the Court of Exchequer. The allegation was that Hugh, being a Catholic, had contravened the Law of obtaining a lease in excess of 31 years. The lease had been taken from John Cole of Florencecourt, Co. Fermanagh. It only needed the proving of the Bill for the property to pass to the 'discoverer.' Kane was so sure of his ground that before the result of the case was known he disposed of his interest in the claim to Hugh Montomery of Derrygonnelly (Margaret's father) with the stipulation that the prosecution he initiated should be pursued. The Court's verdict has not been traced. Undoubtedly it was in the plaintiff's favour. The Kane/Montgomery deed is dated 27th April, 1742. From this it will be seen that Hugh O'Donnell's interest in the Fermanagh lands continued for more than 50 years after the Williamite victory of 1690.

There were only two Catholic families in the townland of Mullaghbane in 1957. Neither had any knowledge or tradition of the O'Donnell sojourn in the place.

Upon coming to Larkfield the O'Donnells became tenants on the Lane/Fox estate. Hugh O'Donnell had a just pride in his name and race. He was a friend and patron of Séamus Maguidhir, an t-Athair Pádraig Ó Corinín and Fergal (or Pádraig) Óg Mac a' Bháird. The last two addressed eulogistic poems to him. He engaged Maguidhir, a noted scribe, to salvage the surviving family poems. Séamus applied himself diligently to the task, searching through old Irish manuscripts and creating an anthology now known as 'Dunaire Uí Dhomhnaill' or 'The Poem Book of the O'Donnells.' The bulk of the work was completed towards the end of May 1727 - a few additions being made at a later date. There are 114 poems in all. Of these 97 are addressed to various members of the O'Donnell family. One laments the death of Flora Hamilton in 1716. Another mourns the passing of Rory of Lifford's son, Col. Manus O'Donnell (26), of Newport, Co. Mayo, that occurred in 1736.

The manuscript is written in a clear hand on ruled paper. The scribe provides a preface and has set out Hugh's pedigree going back through seven generations to Manus Ó Domhnaill, 21st Chieftain (1537-63). The whole comprises an octavo volume, roughly bound in calf. Maguidhir has left it on record that he was handsomely rewarded for his labours.

It is not known when, or how, this priceless work passed out of the O'Donnell family. It was in the possession of Rev. Dr. Paul O'Brien, Professor of Irish at St. Patrick's College. Maynooth, who loaned it to Edward O'Reilly, another noted scholar. Eugene O Curry had access to it in 1857 and appended some notes to the text. It figured as item No. 1438 in the Todd Sale Catalogue of 1869 and found its way into the collection of Sir Thomas Phillips, Bart. The National Library of Ireland had the good fortune to acquire it by purchase from the Phillips Library, Cheltenham, in 1930/1.

Hugh, now resident in Larkfield was looked upon as a person of status and learning. He was known locally as 'Earl O'Donnell,' an appellation that pleased him and which he strove jealously to maintain. The term had been applied by poets to his father's older brother and himself. Hugh was obsessed with being a lineal descendant of the Earl of Tyrconnell. Why he persisted in this absurdity, when it was clear from Maghuidhir's pedigree in an 'Dunaire' that his ancestor was An Calbhach (Chief 1563-6), the Earl's uncle and not the Earl himself, is difficult to understand.

Toirdealbhach O Cearbhallain, the famous harper, was a frequent visitor at Larkfield. Hugh was offended when he learned that 'Hawk of Ballyshannon' composed by Toirdealbhach, referred to a member of the Newport Branch and not to himself 'as lineal descendant of the Earl of Tyrconnell.' In consequence 'the accustomed hospitalities of Larkfield were interdicted to the bard' until an apology was made.

This egoism could have stemmed from the family possessing the actual Patent of 1603/4 creating Rory O'Donnell Earl of Tyrconnell. While the Earldom had been forfeited by attainder the Patent relating to it most likely survived among the Larkfield O'Donnells. It is still in existence.

Richard Pococke, Protestant Archbishop of Dublln, was much impressed by Hugh O'Donnell, whom he met at dinner at Col. Foliot's house ln Ballyshannon on 26 July, 1752. The cleric records in his Journal: 'they say (he) is the head of that (O'Donnell) family descended from the Earl of Tyrconnell and that he has only leases, yet he is the head of the Roman Catholics in this country, and has a great interest, is a sensible man and well vested in the Irish history, both written and traditional.' The Larkfield man's wide knowledge was appreciated by Charles O'Connor of Belangare when he sought his attestation of the genealogy of Count John O'Rourke that he had compiled. Hugh was pleased to oblige, dating his reply from Larkfield on 18th November, 1754, and signing it 'O'Donnell.' Ten days later he was dead.

The Franciscans were brought to Donegal by Nuala O'Brien, wife of Hugh Roe O'Donnell (Chief 1461 - 1505). Her sister, Margaret, invited the monks from there to Creevelea Abbey, Dromahair, Co. Leitrim. Maire, sister of Red Hugh (Chief 1592 - 1602) and wife of Sir Teige O'Rourke, presented a beautiful chalice to the new foundation for the good of her husband's soul. It is now in the Catholic Church, Butlerstown, Co Cavan.

With this long and close association with the Franciscan Order it was natural that the O'Donnells should seek Creevelea, rather than Cloonlougher cemetery, in the parish of Kilargue, right beside Larkfield, as their position would have entitled them to the greatest place of honour within the hallowed walls, but, as it was many years before the occasion arose and as all the internal allocations had been taken up, they had to be content with an outside plot in the angle between the west side of the south transept and the nave. It was here that Hugh was laid to rest. A large elevated, horizontal slab, bearing the O'Donnell Arms, Supporters, Coronet and Motto 'In Hoc Signo Vinces,' with the inscription

> Prey for the soul of O'Donnell Hugh
> Who De parted this life Novr. ye 28th
> 1754 aged 63 yrs.

marks his grave. It is known locally as 'the Earl's Tombstone.'

Hugh's first wife, Flora Hamilton, died 12 November 1716. His second lady, Margaret Montgomery, lived to be 110 years dying in 1795.

Flora's children were: Conall (Karl) (122), John(122a) and Susanna (122b). Her brother, General Count Hamilton, of the Imperial Service, invited his two nephews to Vienna and placed them in the army of Austria, where distinguished careers awaited them. Susanna married Col. Edward Purcell who was serving in Austria.

Karl became Colonel Proprietor of his own regiment, to which he gave his name, in 1756. He rose to the rank of General, became Inspector-General of Cavalry a Privy Councilor and Governor of Transylvania. He was conferred with the
Grand Cross of the Military Order of Marie Therese for his bravery at the Battle of Torgua, 1761. He fought in eighteen battles, was wounded a number of times and died, unmarried, in Vienna on 26th March, 1771, at the early age of 56 years. John commenced his service in 1736, to finally become a Lieutenant-General. He too saw much active service and won the small Cross of the Military Order of Marie Therese at the Battle of Maxen in 1759. He later became Governor of the Elizabeth Theresian Institute, Vienna, dying in that city on 12th March, 1784, aged 72 years. His only son, Hugh (123), a Major, was killed in action at the Battle of Neerwinden ln 1793. He was unmarried. Karl and John were subsequently joined by their step-brother, also John (30a), and relatives from both Newport and Castlebar, until eventually nine Irish-born O'Donnells held commissions in the Austrian Service.

One was required to prove one's sixteen quarterings before being admitted to the Austrian Court. This presented a problem to the O'Donnells owing to the absence of native records. The difficulty was overcome by producing Rory O'Donnell, Earl of Tyrconnell's Patent of 1603/4. It was accepted as proof of nobility and they were given the courtesy title of 'Count.' Several years were to pass before they were elevated to the Imperial Peerage. It came as a reward to Col. Maximilian Count O'Donnell (59) who, as aide-de-camp to the Emperor, saved His Majesty from assassination in 1853.

Hugh and Margaret Montgomery's children were: Con of Larkfield (from whom Fr. Hugh O'Donel, O.F.M., the present Chief of the Name is descended); John who joined his stepbrothers in Vienna and died there young and unmarried; and two daughters, Grace and Kate that married in Co. Fermanagh.

I visited Creevelea Abbey in April 1968 and was both shocked and grieved to find the masonry supporting the 'Earl's Tombstone' had crumbled, leaving the slab lop-sided. Furthermore, the adjoining upright marble monument commemorating later O'Donnells had fallen from its limestone base and lies prone. Its inscription cannot now be read. A small cross that adorned the top is broken off and missing. Rupert S. O Cochlain.

The 'Earl's Tombstone'(shown in photo) lies flat on the ground. Top half shows O'Donnell Arms with arm issuing from right. Arms supported by Lion on left side and Unicorn (?) on right. A coronet (quite weathered and unclear) and mantle appear above, and the motto below.

I visited the 'Earl's Tombstone' on the 11th Feb. 2007.

The marble monument referred to above by Rupert is once again erect and can be read. The inscription reads –

In Hoc Signo Vinces

**In loving memory of
John O'Donnell J.P.
Of Larkfield, Co. Lietrim
Who departed this life 1st October 1874
Aged 73 years
Also of his son
Hugh Neil O'Donnell J.P.
Of Larkfield
Who died 21st Sept. 1887
Age 42 years
And also his son
Captain John O'Donnell D.L., M.B.E.
Who died at Larkfield
15th April 1932
Age 70 years**

The small cross is still missing.
Editor

GODFREY O'DONNELL CHIEFTAN 1248-'58

An extract from a talk given by the late Patsy O'Donnell at Conwal Graveyard during the 1989 Clan Gathering.

Now let me dwell for a moment or two on the famous Godfrey O'Donnell. The well known sepulchral slab in this graveyard has always been regarded as Godfrey's gravestone. From time to time it has been on different locations within these surrounds. There is no valid reason for questioning the verdict of tradition. His castle consisted of clay and timber and probably stood nearby because the O'Donnells had not yet established themselves at Scarbh Sholais. His father was Dómhnall Mór (d. 1241). The achievements of the death of Godfrey would form the subject of a great epic.

In 1247, Malachy, or Mac Lochlann O'Donnell, son of Dómhnall Mór and brother of Godfrey, was slain by Maurice Fitzgerald in battle at Ballyshannon. The country was then spoiled and plundered by the English and they appointed
Roderick O'Canannain to the Government of Tír Chonall. Within a year their covenant with Roderick was violated and
Maurice Fitzgerald and the English marched with a great force to Assaroe on the invitation of Godfrey O'Donnell.
Roderick opposed them, but he was not sufficiently supported by the people of Tír Chonaill. Obviously the majority of the chiefs regarded Godfrey as the legitimate heir to the chieftaincy, and treated O'Canannain as usurper, but both they and Godfrey were playing into the hand of the wily invader. During the next year Maurice Fitzgerald led his forces into Tír Chonaill, which he plundered and devastated. He banished Roderick O'Canannan into Tír Eoghain and left Tír Chonaill in the hands of the great Godfrey.

In 1257, a brilliant battle was fought by Godfrey O'Donnell, now Lord of Tír Chonaill, against Maurice Fitzgerald, now Lord Justice of Ireland, and the English near Sligo Town. A fierce bloody conflict took place. Heroes were disabled and the strength of both sides exhausted. However, Godfrey's men maintained their ground and completely overthrew the English forces. But here unfortunately, Godfrey himself was severely wounded, having encountered in the fight, Maurice Fitzgerald in single combat in which they desperately wounded each other. As usual, the O'Neills, chieftains of Tír Eoghain, had always taken advantage of the weaknesses of the O'Donnells. Brian O'Neill, Lord of Tír Eoghain, took advantage of the dying Godfrey, and in the month of January 1258 sent a messenger to Godfrey demanding -
1 That Godfrey should personally acknowledge his submission and obedience to Brian and,
2. That the Clan should send him hostages to guarantee what he termed 'the continued obedience.'

However, the dying Godfrey would never submit to these terms and he summoned his entire armies to stand and do battle for the country he loved so well. They encountered

O'Neill's forces near the Swilly and fought each other without respect for friend or relative. In the end O'Neill withdrew acrimoniously leaving behind horses and supplies and of course many dead and wounded. As the cry of 'Ó Domhnaill Abu' was heard over the battle ground, the soul of Godfrey was ascending to the throne of Almighty God, and his body was interred in the sacred ground on which we stand.

Stone marking, Godfrey's Grave in Conwal graveyard which is about two miles west of Letterkenny on the Fintown road.

The Battle of Farsetmore

by V. O'Donnell

When Shane O'Neill (the Proud) became Chief of the O'Neills in 1559 he was not content with the Lordship of Tyrone but considered the sovereignty of Ulster his birthright as he claimed descent from the High Kings of Ireland. But before he could assert his dominance, he had many enemies to contend with: members of his own family, neighbouring clans and Queen Elizabeth whose eyes were set on the sovereignty of Ireland.

Shane invaded Tyrconnell in 1557 but O'Donnell (4) had surprised his camp and routed him. Two years later Shane captured Calvagh O'Donnell (4) and his wife Catherine McLean. Calvagh was held prisoner till his release in 1561. After Calvagh's death in 1566 his brother, Hugh Dubh (5), succeeded him as Chief of Tyrconnell and one of his first acts was to raid Tyrone. In 1557 he attacked again and ravaged the whole neighborhood of Strabane.

Shane retaliated. Mustering a large army he marched to the southern shore of the Swilly estuary. Hugh Dubh O'Donnell was at Ardingarry on the other shore with a small body of men.

He immediately sent messengers to summon his forces. But by next morning (8th. May, 1567) none had arrived when the Tyrone men advanced in squadrons of horse, and battalions of foot, towards Farsetmore which lay below Ardingarry.

The river is tidal for some distance above Farestmore, but this being the hour of low water, O'Neill's army passed over the sandbank without difficulty.

O'Donnell prepared his little force and, taking the footmen himself, made off across flat ground to a position amid bogs where he was secure from attack. He had sent his horsemen under the command of his Uncle, Hugh, known as Aodh Mac Aodh Dubh (3) of Ramelton, towards the ford to delay O'Neill's progress. The Ramelton man attacked the Vanguard of O'Neill's cavalry. Many notables fell on each side. But O'Neill was superior in numbers and, noting that his nephew had reached his objective in the bog; Aodh mac Aodh Dubh rejoined him to await the arrival of their supporters.

Soon they were joined by MacSweeney Doe, later by MacSweeney Bannagh. O'Neill by this time had pitched camp to the north of the estuary at Ardingarry. O'Donnell's men, now much reinforced, descended on O'Neill. The latter drew out his force to meet them. Once again, as with so many Irish battles, all detail is lost. Weapons used were: axes, spears, swords, javelins and bows. Gunners were also present. Helmets were worn and round shields were carried.

Horsemen in Irish battles appear to have fought separately from the infantry as much evidence of class distinction as a matter of tactics – and they fought to the left of the infantry. Mercenary soldiers – Galloglaigh – were not always easy to get and we are told of Shane that 'he armeth and weaponeth all the peasants of his country' and that he was the first Irishman to do so. They were called Bonnacht .
"Bonnacht and Gallowglass throng from each mountain pass."

The two armies fought for some hours but in the end O'Neill's men began to draw back pursued by O'Donnell. They made for the estuary but by now the tide had risen and the sand was covered. It was a choice of either facing O'Donnell fury or struggle to the safety of the far bank. Many opted for the latter but to their horror found it too deep to wade. 300 is the estimate of Shane's losses, killed or drowned. The Tyrconnell men had the spoils of victory - horses, arms and military equipment. Shane escaped along the north side of the river, crossed the river near Scairbh Sholais and made his way back to Tyrone. It was to be his last battle. No sooner did he arrive home than he received news of the Lord Deputy advancing against him at the head of a powerful army. Shane fled to the MacDonalds of Antrim and sought their aid, but they hadn't forgotten the past and the result was that Shane's head was severed and delivered to Dublin Castle where it was exhibited over the main gateway.

The remains of those who died at Fearsetmore were buried in Conwal grave-yard along with Godfrey O'Donnell who was buried there three hundred years earlier.
[Sources: Irish Battles by Hayes-McCoy, AFM]
(Farsetmore is the Gaelic for Big Ford).

Manus O'Donnell 21st Lord of Tyrconnell

by V. O'Donnell

Manus, the son of Aodh Dubh (20th Chieftain) was born probably about 1490. He lived at a time of great change when the old Gaelic way of life was under constant attack from the feudal system and treachery, violence and family disloyalty were rife. Being a fierce and tough soldier he was well able for the difficulties surrounding him as he was soon to prove.

In 1510 he was left in charge of Tír Chonaill while his father went on a pilgrimage to Rome. Quite soon his country was attacked by an O'Neill army but Manus, with the help of the McSweeneys, defended it so well that the Tyrone men returned home without success. A few years later Manus had his revenge with the aid of his father and 1,500 gallowglasses he plundered Tyrone as far as Dungannon and made O'Neill give up his claim to Inishown and Kinel Moen (the Lagan country of East Donegal).

What has been described as the bloodiest battle ever between Cineal Chonaill and Cineal Eoghain was fought at Cnoc Buí (Knockavoe) near Strabane in 1522. Manus was defending his base at Lifford against an O'Neill (retaliatory) attack. It ended in great victory for Manus – over 900 of O'Neill's army were killed and much booty taken.

O'Neill was back seeking revenge a few years later but in vain. Manus with the help of more gallowglasses beat off the combined forces of O'Neill and the Lord Deputy (Garret Oge). In 1526 Manus and his father once again invaded Tyrone and took much booty.

In 1527 Manus built a magnificent castle at Port-na-dTrí-Namhad at Lifford It was of stone with a wooden superstructure and he often had to beat off the O'Neills who made every effort to obstruct the building.

The last years of his father's life were difficult for Manus. His half-brother, Aodh Buí, was a rival for the Chieftainship and for several years they fought each other. Aodh Dubh died in 1537 and Manus managed to have himself inaugurated as Chieftain in his place. Aodh Buí died the next year and this left the field clear for Manus who was entering on the most critical period of his career.

As well as being a great soldier he was also fond of literature and even composed some poetry. He caused the 'Life of Colmcille' (his kinsman) to be compiled from the many sources then available. While wooing the Lady Eleanor Fitzgerald, a sister of Garret Oge, he penned the following lines.

Uaimse ag inghin an Iarla
Truaigh gan iasacht mo chroidhe
Go dtuigeadh fein nach bhfeadar
Breagadh croidhe i mbi toirse.

which have been translated thus –

The daughter of a certain Earl
My heart may freely borrow
'Twill teach a lesson to the girl
Who lured me to my sorrow.

She married him eventually only because she believed he would help her to protect a boy, the last of the Fitzgeralds, from the clutches of Henry VIII who had shortly before killed six of the family. But she soon suspected that her husband was planning to hand over the boy for certain favours and so she had the boy smuggled out to France and she herself went back to her own people.

Manus, however, did come to terms with the English. He met St. Ledger, the Lord Deputy, who described him as being the best dressed Irishman he had ever seen, wearing 'a coat of crimson velvet with aglets of gold and over that a great double cloak of bright crimson satin guarded with black velvet and a bonnet with a feather set full of aglets of gold; we thought it strange to see him so honourable and all the rest of his nation that I have seen yet so vile.'

Manus accepted Henry VIII's policy of 'surrender and regrant' but this same policy meant very little in a remote area such as Tír Chonaill. Indeed Manus was to have more trouble from within his own family for the remainder of his life than from the English. He defeated his son, Calbhach, in 1548 at a battle near Ballybofey. In 1555, with the help of some Scottish mercenaries Calbhach took his father prisoner and made himself a de facto Lord of Tír Chonaill. Manus spent several years as his son's prisoner and very unhappy years they were as he expresses in the following lines -

Is cuid de na saobhaidh saobha
Is iad araon ' n mbeathaidh
Ó Domhnaill ar an gCalbhach
'S gan ach Maghnus ar a athair.

Calbhach gained little by his unfilial behavior. His brothers resented his conduct and with the help of Sean O'Neill (Seán an Díomais) they captured and imprisoned Calbhach.

Manus's freedom was short lived. He died early in 1563 at his mansion at Lifford and was buried in the Franciscan Monastery of Donegal. He had led a stormy life with a very mixed experience of triumphs and disasters. The contradictions of his character are well summed up in the obituary written by the Four Masters.

"A man who never suffered the chiefs who were in his neighbourhood to encroach on any of his possessions, up to the time of his decease and infirmity; a fierce, obdurate, wrathful and combative man towards his enemies until he had made them obedient to him; and a mild, friendly, benign, amicable, bountiful and hospitable man towards the learned, the destitutes, the poets and ullamhs, towards the orders of the church as is evident from the old people and historians, a learned man skilled in many arts, gifted with a profound intellect and the knowledge of every science."

[Source; Donegal Annual 1962, AFM]

Mánus a' Phíce

by V. O'Donnell

The story of Manus a' Phíce has been told for generations around Donegal firesides and no wonder for he gained a great victory over his enemy under the most adverse conditions. Happening, as it did, at a time when the Gael were being suppressed, it provided much needed inspiration and morale.

Manus O'Donnell was born near Kilmacrennan, Co. Donegal in 1758. He was a descendant of the Inis Saile O'Donnells whose progenitor was Sean son of Mánus Óg (6).

Manus was educated for the priesthood, but found the call to arms stronger and eventually became a Captain of the United Irishmen in his own area in 1798. He was informed upon by a spy called McGrath, arrested and jailed in Letterkenny. He was kept for a month, fettered neck and foot in a cold, damp, dark cell with only a piece of bread and a pint of water a day.

He suffered much torture and abuse but would not reveal the identity of his comrades. At one time his cell was filled with hungry rats that actually ate the thongs out of his boots. When his captors failed lo extract the information be these means, they tried bribery and promise of protection, but all to no avail.

He was then removed to Lifford Gaol, where after a long time he was brought before a military tribunal under the presidency of Captain Murray. But they failed to convict him due to lack of evidence; McGrath, the principal Crown witness, withdrew his earlier statement for some reason - a matter which caused much embarrassment to the Authorities.

Manus was a renowned pikeman, and the President now declared he would grant him his liberty if Manus agreed to fight a fully armed and mounted dragoon. Mánus accepted the challenge and a day was set.

The contest was arranged in an open field. Mánus was warned that he was merely to defend himself and was not to make any attempt at his opponent's life, while the dragoon was secretly ordered to kill Manus.

Thousands gathered to witness the contest. Cineall Chonaill prayed and hoped for Mánus, for not alone was he fighting for his freedom but he was also defending the honour and dignity of his race and country.

As the dragoon charged towards him, Mánus swiftly stepped aside and with a quick flick of his pike cut the horse's reins, thus reducing the rider's control. Next time the dragoon approached, Mánus again moved sideways and this time brought his adversary to the ground with his pike.

Mánus was immediately apprehended on Captain Murray's orders and condemned to 500 lashes on the triangle. Fortunately for Manus, Lord Cavan, Commander of the Northern Forces happened to arrive on the scene and on hearing the story ordered the prisoner to be set free. Mánus lived a free man till he died in 1844.

A pike was a popular weapon at the time of the United Irishmen. As guns were almost unavailable to the Gael, pikes were manufactured by blacksmiths all over the country.
With a 12'-14' shaft, a bayonet-like blade at the end and a curved blade at the side, especially designed for cutting horses' reins, they- were quite effective against horsemen as the story demonstrates.
Indeed, shortly after the above incident the Authorities provided their cavalry with chains for attaching to the lower part of the reins that hangs between the horse's neck and the bit.

TO ROME BY BOAT, COACH AND HORSEBACK

A lecture given by His Eminence, Tomas O Fiaich, Cardinal Archbishop of Armagh, at Rathmullan in Sept. 1988.

The following is a synopsis of that lecture; the full text appeared in the **1989 Donegal Annual.**

A year before the 'Flight' Chichester had got word that Rory O'Donnell and Cuchonnacht Maguire, Chief of Fermanagh were planning to depart to the Continent. Maguire left in May 1607 and in Brussels contacted Henry O'Neil1, son of the Earl of Tyrone, who was colonel of the Irish Regiment in the Spanish Army in the Low Countries. With a grant of a thousand pounds from the Archduke Albert governor of the Netherlands, they hired a ship, disguised her as fishing smack and under the command of captain, John Rath sailed from Dunkirk in August 1607. On the 25th of the same month (4th. of Sept. in the modern style calendar) she dropped anchor in Lough Swilly where she remained for nine days. Along with her came Cuchonnacht Maguire, Mathew Tully (O'Donnell's secretary), and Donnchadh O Briain. Upon coming to Lough Swilly Donnchadh landed by night and went immediately to Rory who in turn sent word to O'Neill. O'Neill was in Slane, Co. Meath for a meeting with Chichester at the time. By the 8th of September he was on his way stopping at Armagh where he collected the Altar Plate of Armagh Cathedral and brought it with him for safekeeping to Louvain. This collection survived until 1741 but its whereabouts is unknown today. So hasty was O'Neill's departure that he left behind his youngest son, Conn, who was out on fosterage and could not be contacted in time.
Hugh made a speedy journey, meeting with Caffir O'Donnell at Ballindrait and together they arrived at Rathmullan on the 14th September. Caffir's second son, also Conn, did not turn up in time and eventually they left without him. Therefore we can appreciate the urgency and the hard decisions that had to be made before the 'Noble shipload' was ready to sail.
Having taken on board sufficient supplies of food and water, they sailed at noon on Friday, 14th September, the Feast of the Holy Cross. Altogether there were ninety nine people whom we divide into four groups -

(1) Over thirty men and women who finally reached Rome.
(2) Twenty more consisting of children with their teachers and nurses who remained in Flanders.
(3) Twenty three who joined the Irish Regiment in the Spanish Army.
(4) Seventeen, some priests and some clerical students who remained in Flanders to join the Irish seminaries there like Louvain and Douai.

Having sailed down Lough Swilly they headed west where they saw their last sight of Tyrconnel. Going down the west coast of Ireland they kept well off shore to avoid the English ships at Galway but by so doing ran into very stormy weather that lasted 17 days. O'Neill, we are told, had a gold cross which contained a relic of the true cross and this he trailed in the water behind the ship, and according to O Cianain, it gave some relief from the storm. The normal journey from Ireland to Coruna should have taken only four or five days but they were over fourteen days on board ship when nearing the Spanish coast on Sunday 30th September the wind began to blow directly against them and made it impossible to sail for Spain. Instead they were blown up the English Channel, past the Channel Isles and after many adventures and with their stores depleted, the seasick passengers made a landing on the 4th of October, the Feast of St. Francis, near the mouth of the Seine in the little port of Quillebeuf.

Here they were well received by the Governor of the town but he was reluctant to allow them to travel through Normandy without the King's (Henry IV of France) permission. So their interpreter, Mathew Tully, was sent post haste to Paris to meet the King. Meanwhile the English Ambassador, Sir George Carew, requested the King to have them arrested and sent to England. The King, finding himself in a spot, compromised. He did not allow them to travel through France to Spain but granted them permission to go to Spanish occupied Flanders.

That they did - it took over a month, (4th October - 9th November) to reach Louvain. After leaving Quillebeuf, the first big city they encountered was Rouen at the month of the Seine. Then they travelled to Amiens and Arras (by now they were in Spanish Netherlands, today Arras is in France) where they were met by Doctor Eugene McMahon, Bishop of Clogher and later Archbishop of Dublin.

From Monday to Friday (22 - 26th October) they stayed at Douai with its twin Catholic seminaries. Here they received a tumultuous welcome as they were held as popular heroes by the students. On the 23rd the Earls were invited to the English seminary where they were warmly welcomed and entertained at a banquet.
Two of the distinguished Irish Franciscans of the time, Fr. Florence Conry founder of St. Anthony's Louvain and Fr. Robert McArthur of Co. Louth came to Flanders to meet them. From Douai they passed through Tournai and into Halle where O'Neill met his son Henry, who was Colonel of the Irish Regiment. From Halle they were invited to dine in Brussels with the Marquis Spinola, commander of the Spanish Army in the Netherlands and they were also invited to visit the Archduke Albert at his palace at Binche. This visit must have been quite a dramatic one as present was De Lasso a survivor of an Armada wreck twenty years earlier on the Donegal coast, where he saw 300 of his comrades put to death by Henry Hovendon, an

English officer. Those spared, 45 in all, including De Lasso were force-marched to Dublin by Earl Rory's father, Aodh Dubh, and handed over to the authorities there. De Lasso and a few other high-ranking officers were exchanged for English prisoners in Spain. Here now at this meeting were de Lasso, Earl Rory and Henry Hovendon who had since come over to the Irish and was O'Neill's secretary.

From Fri. 9th Nov. - Sun. 25th Nov. they spent in Louvain, then about 40 of the men set out on horseback for Rome where they hoped to go by ship to Spain. They had travelled only 27 miles from Louvain to Namur when they were met by a messenger from King Philip of Spain ordering them to send their plans in writing and await his reply in Flanders. England and Spain had just made peace and Philip hoped to prolong it by avoiding trouble with England but at the same time he didn't wish to alienate himself from the Earls as he would wish Ireland on his side if circumstances changed.

After their initial disappointment, they settled down to spend the winter there. From here we are told they visited places of special interest. The river Schelt was frozen over that winter and they saw about 20,000 people enjoying themselves on the ice.

As the new year came they were under pressure from the Archduke to move on. He didn't wish to offend the English any longer. On Thurs. 28th February they began their long journey once again: 32 men on horseback with a carriage for the women. However the road was so bad that they had to abandon the carriage at Namur after 40 miles and the women too took to horseback. Inside a week they had crossed into Lorraine where they were entertained by the old Duke of Lorraine at his palace at Nancy. By the middle of March they passed into Switzerland and arrived in Basle, the first big protestant city they had encountered. The change was noticeable, says O Cianain, "the inhabitants are heretics," "Teampaill ro-mhoir ina bhfuil dealbhai de Luthar agus Calvin agus droch udair diobhailai eile."

They then moved on till they reached Lake Lucerne where they took to boats and sailed to the southern shore. On St. Patrick's Day in the middle of the Alps occurred the worst accident of the journey. While crossing the Devil's Bridge (Die Teufelsbrucke) which spans a deep gorge on the river Reuss near Fluelen, one of O'Neill's horses carrying most of his wealth panicked and fell into the cascading flood far below. While a few men made their way cautiously down the snowy ravine the rest continued on their journey. But no trace of the money was found. According to O Cianain, this was a serious blow to O'Neill. The amount lost was one hundred and twenty pounds, estimated to be worth about five thousand pounds today.

A week later they came down and out of the Alps on the Southern side and travelled to Lake Lugano where they made their second boat journey and reached Milan on the 23rd. March 1608. They were now on Spanish territory once again and spent a fortnight there. Here they were generously received by the Spanish Governor, Count de Fuentes; visited the Cathedral of Milan and stayed at the hostelry called "The Three Kings," this hotel is still there today.

From Milan to Rome still required a fortnight, they passed through Lodi, Piacenza, Bologna with its great fountain squirting water in the air as it still does today. Friday 18th April they reached the Adriatic at Remini and Catolica. They were now within a few days of Rome which they eventually entered through the Porta del Popula on the 29th. April 1608 and immediately went to pray in St.Peter's Basilica. Thus their journey was completed.

In summing up, the lecturer said, they had travelled approximately 1200 miles since landing on the Continent. That was an average of 40 Kilometers a day - 55 was the longest they had covered in any one day with the exception of their boat journeys. They were all armed and on a few occasions were escorted. Seemingly they had no difficulty obtaining lodgings. They were received graciously and with honour in most towns they passed through; some times they were met outside the cities by governors and some times escorted on leaving. They were shown all the important sites, provided with entertainment of all sorts, saw some of the finest scenery in Europe and saw many of the artistic treasures of the time. As for shrines and relics they had a grand tour of these all along the way and especially in Rome, e.g. the head of John the Baptist, two thorns from the crown of thorns, the nail that went through Christ's feet, a piece of the plate on which was written 'Jesus of Nazereth King of the Jews', portions of the true cross, the cross beam of the cross of the good thief, and many more.

Now, what about those left behind? O'Neill's youngest son, Conn who was left behind was shortly afterwards arrested by the authorities. Chichester proposed that he, along with the son of Caffir O'Donnell should be sent "to some remote part of England or Scotland to be kept from the knowledge of friends and acquaintances or should be dispatched to the plantation of Virginia." In 1615 Conn O'Neill was removed to Dublin, transferred to England where the King sent him to Eton College. In 1622 he was sent to the Tower of London and never heard of again.

Caffir's son, Conn. was more fortunate. Having been held prisoner in Donegal and later in Dublin, he was transferred to England from where he escaped to the Continent. A Donegal tradition claims he returned to end his days in Glenfinn.
Many of those who went with the Earls later pleaded with the English Authorities to allow their wives and families to join them there, and indeed some were successful as the English figured that by their going they were placing an extra burden on Spain and Rome.

The Earls were given a palace in the centre of Rome by the Pope - possibly what is now the Columbus Hotel that you pass on your left as you go into St. Peter's Square. In the days following their arrival they were well entertained and honoured by everyone including the Pope. Eight of them had the honour of carrying the canopy over the Holy Father during the Corpus Christi procession.

Yet the King of Spain and the Pope constantly blamed each other for not being more generous towards the Irish exiles.

Before matters could improve both Rory and Caffir, Maguire and others died in 1608 and were buried in the Franciscan Church of San Pietro in Montorio where their graves can be seen till this day.

Editor's note – I've been told that a carpet covers that floor today, but it may be rolled back upon request to reveal the inscriptions on their graves. The grave next to the O'Donnells is that of young Hugh O'Neill, Baron of Dungannon. V.O'D.

Top left: Fr. Florence Conroy *Right:* Rory and Caffir's grave in Rome.
Bottom Left: Neptune Fountain *Centre:* Colombus Hotel, Rome (residence granted to the Earls),
Right: Devil's Bridge

O'Donnell Participants in the "Flight of the Earls"

by V. O'Donnell

The peace that followed the Treaty of Millifont 1603 was an uneasy one for the northern Chieftains. It soon became obvious that the English had no intention of keeping their side of the bargain and that they wouldn't rest until the Irish leaders were eliminated. With the utmost secrecy, the Chieftains planned their departure. That same departure has wrongfully been called, 'The Flight of the Earls,' for 'Flight' it was not but rather a tactful withdrawal to a place of refuge until such time as they could return with Spanish aid, and confidence to rid Ulster of the 'Gall.'

On the 4th September 1607 a ship put into Rathmullen Harbour under the guise of a fishing boat. Nine days later she sailed down Lough Swilly bearing with her the cream of Irish nobility, Hugh O'Neill, Chief of Tyrone; Rory O'Donnell (13), head of Clann Dálaigh and Cuchonnacht Maguire, Chief of Fermanagh with their respective family, friends and followers - ninety nine in all.

"A distinguished crew was this for one ship; for it is certain that the sea never carried, and the winds never wafted from the Irish shores, individuals more illustrious or noble in genealogy, or more renowned for deeds of valor, prowess, and high achievements." (Annals of the Four Masters).

Here follows a list of those who traveled with **Rory**.
Cathbharr (Cafair (14)) Rory's younger brother, married to Rose Doherty of Inishown with two sons, Hugh and Conn. Conn was left behind due to the urgency of their departure. Cathbharr died in Rome a year later and is buried along with his brother, Rory, in the Franciscan Church of San Pietro de Montorio.
Rose Doherty born 1590, married to Cathbharr above at 14 years. She was a sister of Sir Cathaoir Ó Dochartaigh who rebelled and was killed in 1608. She departed Rome in 1612 and returned to Flanders where she married Eoghan Rua O'Neill. She died in St. Anthony's College, Louvain and is buried there. She was in receipt of 80 crowns a month of a pension from the King of Spain.
Hugh(son of Rory(13)), Baron of Donegal, born 1606. He received 100 escudos of a grant from Spain. He was adopted by Albert, Archduke of Flanders, and called Hugh Albert. Hugh was educated in Louvain. He served in Court where he was known as, "Conde de Tyrconnell" after his father's death. He was in receipt of 100 crowns a month from the King of Spain. He was made colonel of an Irish regiment in the Spanish Army in 1632. In the same year he married Anne Margherrite de Boussu, daughter of Count de Boussu. Hugh was drowned near Barcelona during a sea battle against the French in 1642.
Hugh (son of Cathbharr (14)), born 1605, was fostered at the time of departure but unlike his brother, Conn, was got on board on time. He was left in Louvain in 1608 along with his cousin Hugh (son of Rory (13)) with two Donegal women to take care of them. He was in

receipt of 60 escudos a month from Spain. He joined the Spanish Service, became Captain and fought at Bergh and Breda. He died in 1625 and was buried in front of the high altar in St. Anthony's College, Louvain where is mother was later buried.

Nuala (15) sister of Rory and Cabharr. She deserted her husband, Nial Garbh (16), in 1600 when he went over to the English. She went to Rome along with the main party but was left sad and lonely after the deaths of her two brothers. Nuala returned to Louvain in 1611. She was in receipt of 60 crowns a month from the King of Spain, it was later increased to 175. It is not known when she died but she was living in Flanders at the time of her husband's death in 1626.

Dónal Óg (son of Dónal (10), Red Hugh's half brother) remained in Louvain in 1608 and joined the Spanish Service. He was Captain of the O'Neill Regiment when he was killed in 1620 or 1623.

Neachtain (cousin of Rory (13), and grandson of Donnchadh brother of Mánus 21st Chieftain) remained in Louvain in 1608 and joined the Spanish Service.

Eamon Gruama Mac Daibhéid and his wife; Aodh Ó Gallchóir and his wife, Cecilia: these were two women referred to above who cared for the two Hughs (Rory's son and Cafair's son); the husbands took care of the boys' education. The two couples remained in Louvain in 1608. Gallagher received 30 escudos a month from Spain but no mention is made of a pension to McDaid.

Seán Crónin Mac Daibheid was born in Inishown and was one of O'Doherty's followers. He traveled to Rome in 1608 and was still there in 1615. He wrote to Chichester from Rome asking for a pardon and a safe return but was unanswered. His wife, Finnuala O'Doherty and family did not leave Ireland. Seán was in receipt of 45/50 crowns a month of a pension from Spain. After Rory's death he served O'Neill.

Cathaoir (Mac Toimlín) Ó Gallchóir, Cathaoir (Mac Airt) Ó Gallchóir, Toirleach Corrach Ó Gallchóir, Tuathal Ó Gallchóir agus Aodh Óg (mac Thuathaill) Ó Gallchóir all stayed in Flanders and joined the Spanish Army.

Fr. Colman: Tyrconnell's priest.

Matthew Tully was an educated Connaught man. He went to Spain with Red Hugh in 1602 but returned and became Rory's secretary. He went back to Spain in 1605 and was instrumental in planning the departure of the Earls. He traveled to Ireland in the ship that took them away. On their arrival in Rouen, it was he who traveled ahead to Paris and Flanders to announce their approach. He served in the Spanish Navy and was in Madrid in 1610.

Dennis O'Brian: his grandfather was Bishop of Killaloo. Dennis had served with Rory O'Donnell. He went to Spain in 1602. On his return a few years later he was captured and imprisoned in Athlone but escaped and returned to Spain. He was on board the ship when she arrived at Rathmullan and he travelled by night to bring news of the ship's arrival to Rory. He went with them to Rome.

Eoghan Rua Mac an Bhaird (Ward) O'Donnell's poet. He remained in Flanders in 1608 and had a pension of 30 escudos a month. He later went to Rome and probably died there.

Doighre Ó Duigeannain, an educated Roscommon man. He stayed in Flanders and was in receipt of a monthly pension of 20 escudos. He and Eoghan (above) seem to have been responsible for the education of the youths left behind there.

Donnchadh Mac Suibhne (son of Mac Sweeney, Bannagh) remained in Flanders in 1608 and joined the Spanish Army, O'Neill Regiment in 1612. He later returned to Ireland.

David Crawford, a Scotsman who served as Rory's butler. He went to Rome but returned in 1610.

Muiris, Rory's pageboy, traveled to Rome where he died on 3rd August 1608.

Sean MacPhilip, Aonghus Mac Dhuifithe, Uilliam O Loinsigh agus Cathal Ó Broin, four of Rory's attendants who remained in Flanders and joined the Spanish Service.

Gearoid Ó Conchur (O'Connor) and Capt. Seán Ó Conchur: There is nothing known of these two except that Capt. Seán was in the Spanish Army in 1603 and distinguished himself at the Siege of Ostend.

Gearald Fitzmaurice: Nothing definite is known of him.

Henry O'Kelly joined the Spanish Army, O'Neill Regiment.

Fr. Maurice Dunleavy, a Franciscan Priest from Donegal. He traveled to Spain with Red Hugh in 1602. He was Provincial of Irish Franciscans 1609-1612. He signed the introduction to the 'Annals of the Four Masters' in 1636.

Fr. Florence Conry, born 1560, a Roscommon man, studied in Salamanca and entered the Minor Order of St. Francis. He came to Kinsale with the Spaniards in 1601, but returned with Red Hugh in 1602 and attended at his bedside during his fatal illness. He was Provincial of the Franciscans 1606-1609. He established St. Anthony's College of Louvain in 1606, met the Earls at Douai and accompanied them to Rome. He was appointed Archbishop of Tuam in 1609. He spent the rest of his life between Spain and the Netherlands. His death occurred in Madrid on 18th November 1629 and he was buried in St. Anthony's, Louvain in 1654. He is well known as the author of 'Desiderius.'

Fr. Dermot Doolin traveled with the Earls but remained in Flanders to further his studies.

Five students who went to Flanders to study - **Brian Ó Muiríosa, Niallan Mac Daibheid, Donnchadh Ó Cochlain, Brian Ó hEigeartaigh agus Conchur Óg Ó Duibheannaigh** who was ordained to the Priesthood in 1617.

There were several more - servant boys and maids who attended Rory, Cathbharr, Rose O'Doherty and Nuala but their number and names are not reported.

[Source: Imeacht na nIarlaí le Pádraig de Barra agus Tomás Ó Fiaich]

LAMENT FOR THE PRINCES OF TYRONE AND TYRCONNELL

O woman of the piercing wail,
Who mourest o'er yon mound of clay
With sigh and groan.
Would God thou wert among the Gael!
Thou wouldst not then from day to day
Weep thus alone.
'Twere long before, around a grave
In green Tyrconnell, one could find
This loneliness;
Near where Beann-Boirche's banners wave,
Such grief as thine could ne'er have pined
Companionless.

Beside the wave, in Donegal,
In Antrim's glens, or fair Dromore,
Or Killilee,
Or where the sunny waters fall,
At Assaroe, near Erna's shore,
This could not be.
On Derry's plains-in rich Drumclieff-
Throughout Armagh the great, renowned
In olden years,
No day could pass but woman's grief
Would rain upon the burial-ground
Fresh floods of tears!

Oh no!-from Shannon, Boyne, and Suir,
From high Dunluce's castle-walls,
From Lissadill,
Would flock alike both rich and poor.
One wail would rise from Cruachan's halls
To Tara's hill;
And some would come from Barrow-side,
And many a maid would leave her home
On leitrim's plains,
And by melodious Banna's tide.
And by the Mourne and Erne, to come
And swell thy strains!

(Mangan's beautiful translation of Mac an Bhaird's Lament, 'An Bhean a fuair Feall ar an bhFeart.')

The O'Donnell Name Abroad

By Rupert S. O Cochláin

John O'Donnell, my wife's nephew, from Houston, Texas, U.S.A. was called up for National Service during WWII. He elected for the Navy and was directed to report to the base in San Diego, California. During the long train journey he was surprised to hear his name called out many times at a small station, about 45 miles south of Lubbock. He alighted, approached the official and said, 'I am O'Donnell.' He was told that no one was being sought. The name of the station was merely being announced!

When the Panhandle and Sante Fe railroad was being constructed through this rich farming country of West Texas between 1880 and 1900, an Irishman, Thomas S. O'Donnell of Dallas, had the contract for the hiring of workmen to lay down the track. It was then the custom to name the small towns through which the line passed after some local personage or person connected with the railway - hence O'DONNELL. There could not have been more than a few scattered dwellings in the place at the time as it was not descried as a 'town' until 1908.

It was incorporated as a 'City' in 1923 although its population in 1966 was only 1,300 (year 2000: 1,011.)! Nothing is known of Thomas S. O'Donnell beyond the fact that he was an Irishman.

There are other 'O'Donnell' locations in the United States and elsewhere. There is an O'DONNELL railway station in Pennsylvania and a similar one at O'DONNELL WHARF in Maryland, while Wyoming boasts of O'DONNELL SPUR.

The name had travelled to the Philippines before the Spanish/American War of 1898/9. O'DONNEL (one "L") town (also referred to as Paging by the natives) is situated about 50 miles N.W. of Manilla, in the province of Tarloc.

CAMP O'DONNEL was set up here by the Japanese during the Pacific War. Prisoners taken on Corregidor and Bataan were confined there until their liberation.

The name O'DONNELL is inscribed on the base of the lighthouse in Havanna Harbour, Cuba. It dates from the time of

Gen. Leopoldo O'Donnell y Joris who was governor of the Island from 1844-48.

There is a CALLE (street) O'DONNELL in Madrid and other cities in Spain. Madrid also has and an O'DONNELL train station. The old quarter of San Juan, the capital of Puerto Rico in the Caribbean has one, while I have traversed the CALLE O'DONNELL of Ceuta, North Africa.

The name here honours the same Gen. Leopoldo O'Donnell who also commanded the victorious Spanish forces in the Moroccan campaign of 1859-60, thereby earning for himself the title 'Duke of Tetuan.'

O'DONNELL ABU

Proudly the note of the trumpet is sounding
Loudly the war cries arise on the gale;
Fleetly the steed by Lough Swilly is bounding,
To join the thick squadrons in Saimear's green vale.
On, ev'ry mountaineer,
Strangers to fight and fear;
Rush to the standard of dauntless Red Hugh!
Bonnaught and Gallowglass,
Throng from each mountain pass;
On for old Erin, "O'Donnell Abu!"

Princely O'Neill to our aid is advancing,
With many a chieftain and warrior clan;
A thousand proud steeds in his vanguard are prancing,
'Neath the borders brave from the banks of the Bann:
Many a heart shall quail,
Under its coat of mail;
Deeply the merciless foeman shall rue
When on his ear shall ring,
Borne on the breeze's wing,
Tír Chonaill's dread war-cry, "O'Donnell Abu!"

Wildly o'er Desmond the war-wolf is howling,
Fearless the eagle sweeps over the plain,
The fox in the streets of the city is prowling -
All, all who would scare them are banished or slain!
Grasp every stalwart hand
Hackbut and battle brand -
Pay them all back the debt so long due;
Norris and Clifford well
Can of Tirconnell tell;
Onward to glory - "O'Donnell Abu!"

Sacred the cause that Clan Connell's defending -
The altars we kneel at and homes of our sires;
Ruthless the ruin the foe is extending -
Midnight is red with the plunderer's fires.
On with O'Donnell, then,
Fight the old fight again,
Sons of Tirconnell,
All valiant and true:
Make the false Saxon feel
Erin's avenging steel
Strike for your country! - "O'Donnell Abu!"

Ó Domhnaill Abú

Tá buabhaill Chlann Dálaigh go huallach a' séideadh
Agus dordfhionn Thír Chonaill a' dúascadh na ngleann'
Tá eachra Loch Súilí go tinntrí ag léimnigh
Ag tarraingt 'n a' chomhraic go dícheallach teann.
Eirigí 'a chlann na sliabh,
Sibh nach raibh claoite 'riamh,
Bailigí thart ar a' Dálach gan tnúth;
Buanach is Gallóglach,
Réabadh trí shléibhte 'mach
A' scairtigh go bródúil – 'Ó Domhnaill Abú!'

Tá loinnir na lanntrach ag síneadh go líofa
Chomh tiubh leis na fuinnseoga' gcoill Dhún na nGall,
Tá moing ár gcuid eachraí ag siabadh le gaoth uainn
Agus carnadh a gcrúb mór ag réabadh na mbeann.
Réabfar is roisfear linn,

Brisfear is loiscfear linn,
Caisleáin is cathracha is neartmhaire cliú,
Éifeacht ár sinnsear linn,
Crógacht is cinnteacht linn,
Ar aistear na gcuradh linn –'Ó Domhnaill Abú!'

Tá tailte Thír Eoghain ar ár n-aistear ag síneadh
Agus dúiche Uí Chatháin ar an bhealach na nGleann,
Tá tuilte na Banna romhainn ag doirteadh go líon-mhar
Agus dúnta 'gus laochra 'tá teann.
Triallfar na mílte linn,
Cloífear na laochra linn,
Folcfar le hurla ár gcuid sleanntrach le crú'
Feolmhach is fabhairteach,
Dioscarnach, dramhaltach
A dhéanfar go treise linn– 'Ó Domhnaill Abú!'

O'Donnell Abu is probably the best known and most popular O'Donnell song. The tune was composed in the early part of the 19th century by a man from Carrick-on-Suir, Co. Tipperary. His name was Joseph Haliday and he was bandmaster of the Cavan Militia. He died in Dublin in 1846, aged 71 years.

Michael McCann, a young Galway man, added words to the music. The composition first appeared in 'The Nation' of January, 1843 and was then called 'The Clan Connell War Song'. McCann, afterwards emigrated to America but later returned to England. At the time of his death in 1883 he was a shopkeeper in London. A celtic cross marks his grave in St. Patrick's Catholic cemetery.
Years later Seosamh Mac Grianna, Rann-na-Feirsde, did the Irish translation.

Hugh O' Neill and Hugh O'Donnell Roe

In days gone by right royally, o'er fair and wide domain,
Of Ulster lands and mountains grand, green vales and fertile plain;
'Twixt Fanad brown and Augher Town and 'twixt old grey Ardboe
And Inishsail ruled Hugh O'Nale and Hugh O'Donnell Roe.

Then Saxon vile with force and guile all Ulster tried to gain
But ready brands in Irish hands made all their efforts vain,
Well Norris knew and Essex too that they could ne'er o'erthrow
The warlike Gaels led by O'Nale and Hugh O'Donnell Roe.

On Bandon's banks in serried ranks, while sat the wintry sun
Stood stalwart men from every glen 'twixt Larne and Cushendun,
From Swillyside and Keenagh wide, Dungannon and Raphoe,
They were all gathered round O'Nale and Hugh O'Donnell Roe.

At dead of night began the fight 'round that beleaguered town
Where many a kern and trooper stern and armoured knight went down,
'Twas not the crew led by Carew but fate that night of woe
At far Kinsale that crushed O'Nale and Hugh O'Donnell Roe.

One found a grave by Tiber's wave in grand and stately Rome,
While the other found on Spanish ground his final earthly home,
But history will record until the shamrocks cease to grow
The thrilling tales of Hugh O'Nale and Hugh O'Donnell Roe.

(Composer unknown)

O'DONNELL DWELLING PLACES

by V. O'Donnell

The O'Donnells first resided on an island, probably a man-made one (crannóg), in Lough Veagh. But where was Lough Veagh? Here follows an article which appeared in the Donegal Annual 1965.

'The Crannóg of Lough Veagh'
"Since the visit of John O'Donovan here, exactly 130 years ago, most writers have followed his identification of the centuries-old O'Donnell Crannog of Lough Veagh with the little island in Glenveagh Lake. Now this O'Donovan-sponsored doctrine must be abjured, as its error has been proved in a recent piece of research by a Donegal scholar in this journal. From this we learn that Loch Beathach (or Lough Veagh) was the old name for Gartan Lough (just over the hill from Glenveagh) and was known as such to Manus O'Donnell (d. 1564) and his forbears, who had their lake-girt stronghold there for many generations. Here then on this island on Gartan Lough and not in Glenveagh, was O'Donnell's medieval fort. Here was the, scene of Godfrey O'Donnell's historic homecoming on his bier from the decisive victory over the Connacht Normans at Credran, in 1257. Here, we may take it, in the words of Aubrey de Vere:

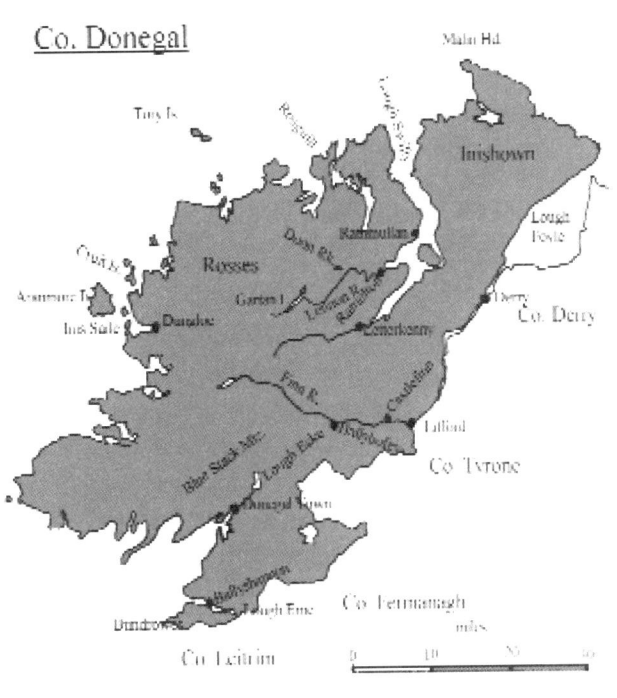

'O'Donnell lay sick with a grievous wound;
The leech had left him, the priest had come,
The clan lay weeping upon the ground,
Their banners furled and their minstrels dumb . . . . !'

From this island fort too, the dying, but dauntless Godfrey, still on his bier, led the Cenel Conaill against the invading Brian O'Neill to win the day at the Swilly in 1258, and there to die and be buried at Conwall, where his tomb is still to be seen. "This," states the Four Masters, "was no death of cowardice, but the death of a hero, who had at all times triumphed over his enemies . . . . ."

Gartan Lough is drained by the Lennon River and it was on the banks of this river, close to where Ramelton stands today, that the O'Donnells had their first permanent home.

Later they built castles or forts at Bundrowes (foundations discovered 2006), Ballyshannon, Lifford, Caoluisce. Castlefinn and Donegal Town.

They also had a fortress, the ruins of which still exist, on an island known as 'O'Donnell Island' in Lough Eske a few miles from Donegal Town. It was here that Aodh Rua (12) imprisoned O'Connor Sligo. O'Connor was released by Rory after Aodh's death.

As Aodh Rua destroyed Donegal before traveling to Kinsale, it was to Lough Eske Castle that Rory returned after the battle. This, tower-house was built on the shore of Lough Eske and it was from here that Rory set out on his journey to Rathmullan to board the ship that took him to the Continent in 1607.

On Rory's departure, his property was confiscated by the English, but his mother Ineen Dubh, seems to have been resettled in the east of the County as we find her shortly afterwards living in Monagavlin Castle on the banks of Lough Foyle. Lifford Castle was occupied by other members of the family until Rory of Lifford (22) was moved to Connaught during the Cromwellian Plantations sometime prior to 1664.

Galún Uí Dhomhnaill

Two versions of the origin of 'Galún Uí Dhomhnaill' (O'Donnell's Gallon) have appeared in the annual of the Donegal Historical Society. A story told by a Cruitman and recorded by Rupert S. O Cochlain says: After spending the day hunting in the Blue Slack Mountains, O'Donnell and a party of huntsmen were returning to Donegal when they stopped at an inn to refresh. O'Donnell called for a gallon of drink but the bar-keeper, being so excited at his noble company produced instead four gallons and a pint. On seeing his mistake, the innkeeper was about to pour back the excess but O'Donnell wouldn't allow it and paid for all the drink. Then he said to his men "Ólaigí gallon Uí Dhomhnaill anois a fhearra." They drank their fill and the remainder was left for thirsty travellers who passed that way.

Niall Ó Dónaill, however states that 'Gallún Uí Dhomhnaill' was a vessel for holding wine and its capacity was 16 quarts, 1 pint and 1 glass which corresponded to the half-anker wine barrels used on the Continent at that time.

To-day when food or drink is offered in abundance it is referred to as 'Gallún Uí Dhomhnaill.'

The Jahrgang O'Donell

by V. O'Donnell

In the year 1736 and at the age of 21 Connell O'Donnell (g.g.g.g.g. grandson of Manus O'Donnell, 21st Chieftain) left his home near Dromahaire in Co. Leitrim and joined his uncle Count Andrew Hamilton in Austria. Many young men who were not prepared to take English oppression did likewise. They are remembered as the 'Wild Geese.'
Connell, known on the continent as Karl, commenced his career in No. 7 Kurassier Regiment during the Turkish War. Rapidly rising through the ranks he was Colonel Proprietor of the O'Donnell Regiment from 1756 to 1771. He was awarded the Grand Cross of the Military Order of Maria Therese in 1761. He became Commanding Officer in the Netherlands in 1762, Counsellor in 1764, Inspector General of Cavalry in 1765 and finally, Privy Councillor and Governor of Transylvania in 1768. He died without issue in Vienna - a veteran of 18 campaigns – on March 26, 1771.

Each Cadet Class graduating from the Maria Theresian Military Academy of Weiner Neustadt (60 Km. south of Vienna) take as patron one of the great Austrian military heroes and the class graduating in 2005 took Karl O'Donnell. Hence they became the 'Jahrgang O'Donell.' Note - the surname in Austria has been spelt with one 'n' since 1853 as the result of a misspelling in a patent granting the title 'Count.'

The Jahrgang O'Donell took a keen interest in the O'Donnell, Donegal and Irish background of their patron and so, many Austrian/Irish events took place during their four year course culminating in a week-long trip to Ireland at the end of August 2005. During that week the 67 cadets along with several senior officers including Major Douglas O'Donell Count von Tyrconnell were hosted by the Irish Army and travelled around visiting scenic and historic sites but the highlight was their visit to Co. Donegal.

While guests of the 28th Infantry Battalion in Finner Camp they were taken to some of the interesting sites of our county such as Bunglass, Rock of Doon and Glenveagh. A very impressive ceremony was held at Donegal Castle where after an oration by Major Douglas O'Donnell, a plaque commemorating their visit was unveiled by Major Douglas O'Donell and Major Norbert Sinn, Commandant of the Military Academy.

Their trip ended with a dinner in Finner Camp at which members of the O'Donnell Clan Association were special guests.

One week later the passing-out took place at the Military Academy. It was a two-day affair with much pomp and ceremony. The Jahrgang O'Donell did much to give it an Irish and an O'Donnell flavour. Two pipers were 'imported' from Ireland, Private Willie Coffey from the Army Barracks at Lifford and Vincent O'Donnell, Inver secretary of the O'Donnell Clan Association. The O'Donnell flag was ceremoniously carried during all ceremonies and the two pipers provided all the music including the march past in the main street of the town where over ten thousand watched including the President, Heinz Fischer and the Minister for

over ten thousand watched including the President, Heinz Fischer and the Minister for Defence, Gunter Platter. A stamp with the Jahrgang O'Donell badge was issued on the day and even the Irish Whiskey had a special label bearing the O'Donnell arms and motto.

The Jahrgang O'Donell with the commemorative plaque in the grounds of Donegal Castle 2nd Sept. 2005.

Unveiling the plaque in Donegal Castle –
Major Douglas O'Donnell Count von Tyrconnell and Major General Norbert Sinn

The badge of the Jahrgang O'Donnell (O'Donell Class)

Joseph (43a)

Alexandro (43b)

Enrique (43d)

Carlos (43)

Ann Stafford, wife of Hugh (55)

Hugh (55)

Hugh Roe (63)

Mary Napier Phibbs, wife of Conn (40)

Arms above No. 2 Mirabel Platz

Count Douxi (360) with Fiacha grandson of Alfonso (70d) at No. 2 Mirabel Platz, Salzburg.

Uniform of O'Donnell Regiment, Austrian Army

Leopoldo (70) during conferring ceremony 1956. Eamonn DeValera was then Chancellor.

Mary Napier Phibbs O' Donnell (55b)

Rose Hannah (55c)

Nuala (64a)

Siobhán (64b)

Leopoldo (70), Carlos (70a), Jóse Luis (70b), Juan Antonio (70c) & Alfonso (70d)

Juan Antonio, Felix & Rafael sons of Juan (70c) with Agustin son of Jóse Luis (70b)

Leopoldo grandson of Jóse Luis (70b)

< Gonzalo grandson of Jóse Luis (70b)

> Patricio son of Alfonso (70d)

Maurice (60)  Joseph (44)  Johannes (76)

Douglas (71)  Henry (37)  Hugo (68)

Gabriel (75)  Charles Farkas (355)  Votive Kirche, Vienna